The Pension Crisis

The Pension Crisis

Robert J. Lynn
The Ohio State University

LexingtonBooks
D.C. Heath and Company
Lexington, Massachusetts
Toronto

Library of Congress Cataloging in Publication Data

Lynn, Robert J.
  The pension crisis.

  Includes bibliographical references and index.
  1. Pensions—United States.   2. Pension trusts—
United States.   3. Pensions—Law and legislation—
United States.   4. Pension trusts—Law and legislation
—United States.   I. Title.
HD7106.U5L94 1983   331.25′2′0973   82–48795
ISBN 0—669-06374-6

Copyright © 1983 by D.C. Heath and Company

All rights reserved. No part of this publication may be reproduced or transmitted in any form or by any means, electronic or mechanical, including photocopy, recording, or any information storage or retrieval system, without permission in writing from the publisher.

Published simultaneously in Canada

Printed in the United States of America

International Standard Book Number: 0–669–06374–6

Library of Congress Catalog Card Number: 82–48795

Contents

	Preface	vii
Chapter 1	**An Introduction to Pensions**	1
	The Context of Pensions	2
	Conclusion	10
Chapter 2	**The Pension Crunch: The Population, the Work Force, and the Retired**	15
	The Demographic Imperative	17
	The Population	20
	Productivity, the Economy, and the Dependency Ratio	29
	Conclusion	30
Chapter 3	**Pension Systems**	41
	Social Security	42
	Private Pensions	48
	Federal-, State-, and Local-Government Pension Plans	52
	Military Pensions and Veterans Pensions	55
	Railroad Pensions	57
	Conclusion	58
Chapter 4	**Pensions in the Changing Wealth-Transmission Process**	65
	The Family	66
	The Contemporary Wealth-Transmission Process	71
	The Context of Wealth Transmission	76
	Improving the Wealth-Transmission Process	78
	Conclusion	81
Chapter 5	**The Employee Retirement Income Security Act (ERISA)**	85
	The Principal Features of ERISA	86
	Private Pension Problems of the 1980s	97
	Conclusion	105

Chapter 6	**Investing Pension Funds**	111
	Legal Constraints	112
	Political Constraints	119
	The Sums at Stake	121
	Conclusion	121
Chapter 7	**Reducing Pension Costs**	127
	Full Employment	127
	Coordinating Benefits (Offsetting)	137
	Indexing	142
	Conclusion: The Prospects for Success	144
Chapter 8	**The Future of Pensions**	149
	Factors Affecting Pension Systems and Pension Benefits	150
	Conclusion	159
	Glossary	165
	Index	171
	About the Author	177

Preface

This book was written for people interested in and affected by the current pension crisis: the disabled and the retired who receive pensions and the millions of people in the work force who forgo some consumption in order to support pensioners and other dependent groups in the population.

Pension systems are commonly misunderstood; thus one purpose of this book is to explain them and to make clear their precarious nature. Another intention of this book is to encourage thinking about pensions in the context of the income-maintenance and wealth-transmission systems of which they are a part. Because components of the income-maintenance system developed on a piecemeal basis, most people tend to think of them separately. Also, because conventional methods of transferring wealth (as gifts and inheritances) are so old and so well established, most people tend to think of them as exclusive and pervasive. In truth, pensions are but one method by which the work force supports the dependent segments of the population, and for the middle class, pensions are displacing more traditional methods such as intergenerational gifts and inheritances.

Although successive chapters build on preceding material in the book, each chapter is structured so that it can be read independently. Therefore, there is some repetition within the book.

The book draws on articles I wrote that were published in the Arizona, Colorado, and Georgia law reviews and the Ohio State law journal. The articles are cited throughout the book. I thank the officers of those publications for permission to use copyrighted material.

I also thank the members of the library and secretarial staffs of the College of Law, The Ohio State University, who assisted me in the preparation of the manuscript.

1 An Introduction to Pensions

With the advent of automation after World War II and the resulting elimination of many manual-labor jobs, the American public pressed for a *guaranteed annual income* to provide for workers whose skills had become obsolete and who had exhausted unemployment-compensation benefits.[1] The massive displacement of workers predicted by some economists, however, simply did not occur. Thus, eventually, the idea of a guaranteed annual income was displaced by the *negative income tax*,[2] a notion that still finds vestigial expression in the Internal Revenue Code as an "earned-income credit"[3] available to a small percentage of the work force.

Although most people shy away from fully supporting a guaranteed income called just that, there is, nonetheless, in the United States a guaranteed income of sorts, consisting of a hodge-podge of benefits made up of money payments, provisions of goods and services, and subsidies supported by federal-, state-, and local-tax structures. Social security and unemployment compensation are familiar, well-established components of this income-maintenance system.[4] Components of the system vary over time, as programs are begun, grow, and (rarely) die. One characteristic persists regardless of the mix: namely, chaos. Plans and programs overlap. Both time and money are spent determining eligibility for, or entitlement to, benefits. Beneficiaries complain of unfair denial of benefits, unconscionable delay in providing benefits, and unjustified termination of benefits. Taxpayers and others supporting programs complain of fraud, inefficiency, and waste. Bureaucrats, who are objects of the wrath of beneficiaries, taxpayers and other contributors, complain of harassment. This state of affairs will persist as long as those in the work force, that is, those who are financing the support system, are willing to forgo some consumption to provide benefits in an inefficient way.

The army of workers engaged in servicing the support system is itself a part of the work force. Improving efficiency in providing an adequate income to all would result in some loss of jobs in the federal-, state-, and local-government bureaucracies, and in banks, insurance companies,

---

This chapter is drawn from R.J. Lynn, *Private Pensions in Perspective: Problems of the Years Ahead,* 15 Ga. L. Rev. 269 (1981). Copyright © 1981 by the Georgia Law Review Association, Inc. Reprinted by permission.

and health-care organizations. Offices of lawyers, accountants, investment advisors, and actuaries would not go untouched. Thus these groups may perceive a streamlining effort as threatening to their jobs and will naturally be reluctant to encourage change.

Pension plans are a part of the income-maintenance system, and they mirror many of the characteristics of the larger system. Some tax-supported benefit programs have expanded dramatically within the last decade, and, similarly, pension plans have grown in importance. Assets of pension plans are of enormous value, and as the changing nature of the wealth-transmission arrangements of middle-class Americans becomes common knowledge,[5] the accumulation, management, and disposition of such assets will be more widely discussed, analyzed, and taught.[6] Pension law that is now of interest principally to practicing lawyers and fiduciaries will be learned routinely by law students as a part of legal literacy. Although the debate continues over that rag bag of benefits encompassed by social security,[7] it does not completely obscure the quieter examination of the development of private pensions and their role and future in the United States.

This chapter first describes in a general way the retirement- and disability-benefit system, of which pensions are but a part. Thereafter, the economic and political importance of pensions is explored, and the criticisms commonly leveled at pensions are listed. Last, the future of the pension device is predicted.

The Context of Pensions

What Is a Pension?

A *pension* is generally considered a payment of money made at regular intervals over a period of time. It is, in short, an *annuity*. The sum receivable might be unvarying in amount *(fixed)*, or it might change because it is *indexed* (that is, tied to a variable such as the consumer price index)[8] or *variable* (that is, dependent on the investment experience of the accumulated funds from which the pension is drawn). The period of time that a pension is payable might be fixed (for example, twenty years), or it might vary (for example, payable for the life of the pensioner).

Although pensions are payable in money, the expectation of both those who receive pensions and those who pay pensions is that the pension payments will be used principally or exclusively to buy goods and services such as food, clothing, shelter, health care, and transportation. That pensions give access to goods and services leads to several observations. First, if the pension receivable does not cover the costs of es-

Introduction to Pensions 3

sential goods and services, the pensioner must either find additional resources to meet such costs or go without. Second, if the pension receivable does cover costs but one or more of the desired goods and services are in short supply, the pensioner must go without, as must his contemporaries. Although his age or disability might induce others to give him priority with respect to goods and services in short supply, experience shows that he seldom is. Last, the right to direct access to goods and services might be more valuable than receiving a pension with which to try to buy them. For example, because veterans pensions are often modest, the right of a veteran to medical attention at a Veterans' Administration hospital might be worth much more to the veteran than the right to a periodic fixed payment based on length of military service.

Viewed realistically, then, a *pension* is a claim to such goods and services as are available for distribution from time to time. The pensioner is supported by the work force through the intricate system of *income transfers* (or *transfer payments*) of which pensions are a part.

The Jargon of Pensions

Not surprisingly, a jargon has developed with respect to pension plans.[9] Much of the jargon is of principal interest to technicians (creators, administrators, or regulators of plans), but some of it is of general interest. A *participant* is a person enrolled in a pension plan, usually a current employee or a retired employee. *Beneficiary* and *covered employee* are terms frequently used interchangeably with *participant*. Participants view a plan as being advantageous to them (1) if it is *noncontributory* (as opposed to *contributory*), that is, if it is a plan funded solely by an employer or group of employers; (2) if it requires early *vesting*, that is, if it gives a right to a pension that does not depend on continuing employment by a participant until retirement age; and (3) if it results in *portability* of pension credits upon a change of employment. (Social security is the outstanding example of a retirement system that includes both vesting and portability of pension credits.) Under an *insured* pension plan, accumulated pension funds are invested and administered by an insurance company; under a *trusteed* plan, accumulated pension funds are invested and administered by a *trustee* (usually, but not always, a bank with trust powers).[10] Some pension plans do not include an accumulation of assets from which to pay pensions; such plans are called *unfunded*. A *qualified* plan is constructed and administered to qualify for tax advantages under the Internal Revenue Code.

Some pension plans specify the pension payable upon retirement or the method of determining the pension. For example, the pension benefit might take the form of a flat sum per month at retirement. Such plans are called *defined-benefit* plans. Some pension plans, on the other hand, fix contributions to the plan but not the pension payable upon retirement. The pension payable turns on what the accumulated fund in a participant's account will buy upon retirement. Such plans are called *defined-contribution plans*.

Who Receives Pensions?

With some exceptions, eligibility to receive a pension depends on being (or having been) a member of a group. Retirement or disability benefits are received principally by (1) persons covered by social security (Old Age, Survivors, and Disability Insurance); (2) federal civilian employees; (3) career military personnel; (4) state- and local-government employees; (5) persons covered by private (corporate or industrial) pension plans; (6) veterans; and (7) railroaders.

Self-employed people are subject to the social security tax law (Federal Insurance Contributions Act) and are therefore eligible for social security benefits irrespective of whether they are (or have been) members of groups. Some self-employed people are beneficiaries of Keogh retirement plans[11] authorized by Congress to put the self-employed who choose to create such plans on an approximate tax parity with employed people covered by *qualified* pension plans (that is, plans accorded favorable tax treatment under the Internal Revenue Code). Self-employed and employed people (although covered by qualified pension plans or government pension plans) are authorized by Congress to create Individual Retirement Accounts (IRAs) accorded favorable tax treatment similar to that given qualified pension plans.[12] In short, although most pensions originate in group membership, some do not. Rather, they originate in an arrangement either requiring or encouraging the creation of pension benefits for those who otherwise might have none.

It bears emphasis that retirement or disability benefits frequently are extended not only to the participant in the plan but also to members of his family. Indeed, it is the extension of benefits to persons other than the participant that is a principal source of the financial difficulties of some retirement systems. The tendency has been to extend benefits first to the surviving spouse of the participant, then to minor children of the participant, and last (and this is somewhat less likely) to other dependents of the participant.

How Large Are Pension Payments?

Just as there is a wide range of individual earned incomes in the United States, so there is a wide range of individual pension incomes. Under many pension systems, pensions payable bear some relationship to both contributions made by a participant (or on his behalf) and the length of time that a participant was a member of a pension plan during his working years. Thus a group member who has earned high income over a long period receives a larger pension upon retirement than a participant who earned less or who worked a shorter period, or both.[13]

Because pension benefits commonly bear some relationship to past earned income and are calculated to produce an income less than earned income, most seldom exceed earned income. Nonetheless, pension benefits exceeding preretirement earned income occasionally are paid.[14] A pension benefit higher than earned income might result from *indexing* —that is, varying the pension benefit in accordance with a variable such as the consumer price index. Or a pension higher than past earned income might originate in a pension system that is unconnected with employment in the usual sense—for example, a pension payable to a veteran is payable because of past service to the United States. Similarly, although pensions payable to a surviving spouse of a participant tend to be proportional to what the participant himself received or might have received had he lived, benefits payable to other dependents might be affected by other variables (for example, the number of dependent children).

Pension benefits are deeply affected by choice of work.[15] Police officers and fire fighters usually receive pensions higher than those of other municipal employees. State- and local-government employees receive pensions that are about one-third larger than those available to employees of private industry. Government pensions at all levels—federal, state, and local—are more likely than industrial pensions to have inflation escalators.[16] Big-company pension plans tend to pay more generous benefits than small-company plans. And many small companies have no pension plans at all.

In short, because there is great variety of pension systems and pension plans, there is great variation in pension benefits paid. Some pensioners do indeed enjoy generous pension incomes, but they are the exception. Although the total sums paid in pensions in the United States today are staggering, most retired, disabled, and dependent people have modest pension incomes.

Income Transfers (Transfer Payments)

Generally speaking, pension systems are part of the income-transfer system by which those in the work force support the dependent segment of the population (the old, the retired, the disabled, the unemployed, the young, and the poor). Thus those earning large incomes share their incomes with those who have smaller or no incomes. Both the support afforded by the work force to the dependent population and the sharing of incomes are usually involuntary.[17] It is true that employees are sometimes given a choice of either participating or not in a pension plan, but very few people gainfully employed in the private sector have any choice in making social security contributions. The progressive income tax that produces most of the federal revenue is also frequently an element of both state- and local-tax systems.

The fact that a pension plan entails contributions by covered employees to a fund does not assure exclusion of the plan from the income-transfer system. Regardless of whether a pension plan is sponsored by government, by an employer, by a union, or by a combination of employer and union, and irrespective of whether it is funded, or unfunded, contributory, or noncontributory, the tendency has been to expand benefits available under the plan, and to extend the plan to new classes of participants (called *blanketing in*). Consequently, although benefits paid have a rough relationship both to contributions made by a participant (or on his behalf) during his working years and to the length of time that the participant was a part of the work force, the relationship is not always directly proportionate. When a new class of participants is blanketed into a pension plan, there might indeed be some entrance fee exacted, but the major cost of blanketing in might have to be borne by those participants already part of the plan at the time that blanketing occurs. When benefits of government pension plans are expanded or extended to new classes of participants, the cost is frequently borne by taxpayers because the costs of some pension systems are payable from general revenues. In other words, although a pension plan could be so constructed that those drawing benefits receive in substance only a return of what they have themselves contributed to the plan, a combination of factors—rising expectations, an extended period of economic prosperity, the politicizing of the pension problem—has resulted in skewing the pension systems away from insurance and toward welfare. Pensioners usually get benefits that are disproportionate to their contributions.

Double-Dipping

That pensions are perceived to be a part of the income-transfer system is shown by the resentment directed toward those who receive pension payments from more than one source.[18] For example, a pensioner during his working years might have been covered by a federal civil-service pension plan. He accumulated credits sufficient to enable him to draw a pension under the rules of the plan. He left federal service and became self-employed, paying social security self-employment tax. At age sixty-five he ceases to work and begins to draw both a civil-service pension and social security retirement benefits (a practice referred to as *double-dipping*). Double-dipping is stoutly defended by those engaged in it. They point with some persuasiveness to the fact that the opportunity to be covered by more than one pension plan is open to all who wish to take advantage of it. And certainly if a person with his own funds were to buy annuities from two insurance companies, he indisputably would be entitled to draw annuity payments from both. If all pension systems were firmly grounded on insurance and actuarial principles, the issue of double-dipping would not arise. The ambiguous nature of so many pension systems has given rise to the problems, including double-dipping, that plague pensions.

The Economic and Political Importance of Pensions

Although it is both conventional and helpful to allude to the vast sums accumulated in public and private pension funds to show their economic and political importance, it might be more illuminating to identify the three principal groups of people affected by pension, health, and welfare systems, irrespective of whether a particular system requires accumulation of funds.

Pensions, whether public or private, are supported by the work force either indirectly through the tax system (for example, veterans pensions) or directly through contributions to pension funds by employers, employees, or both. Until World War II, the work force consisted largely of adult males. Since World War II women have entered the work force in ever increasing numbers. Many working women are married, and many are mothers of minor children. In sum, the work force in the United States today is a mix of men and women, married and unmarried, who in some way support the great variety of pension systems that exist.

About one-half of those in the private work force are covered by private pension plans.[19] About three-fourths of all government civilian employees are covered by pension plans other than social security. Nongovernmental employees, the self-employed, and the armed forces are covered by social security. For noncareer military personnel, there are pensions for veterans. In short, rich and poor, civilian and soldier, old, middle-aged, and young—nearly all are affected directly by the proliferation of pensions, and the few not affected directly nonetheless are affected indirectly.[20]

People who receive pensions are principally the old and the mentally or physically disabled. Many are widows of deceased participants. It bears emphasis, however, that minor or disabled children of deceased or disabled participants are included among the beneficiaries of pension plans, as are participants who themselves retired early in middle age and either ceased to work altogether or remain in the work force (sometimes for the specific purpose of qualifying for a pension from a second source).

In addition to those who support pension systems and those who receive pension benefits, there is a third group affected by pensions consisting of those who *service* pension, health, and welfare systems. Some who service systems are government employees—the most obvious being employees of the U.S. Department of Health and Human Services who administer the social security system. But many who service systems are drawn from the professions, from business, and from industry—accountants, actuaries, lawyers, bankers, insurers, investment counselors, administrators, investigators, and clerks. They collect funds from the work force to support pension, health, and welfare systems. Where systems are funded, they invest and reinvest accumulated funds. They process claims to benefits, and they ultimately distribute pension payments or supervise provision of services in kind.

There is of course overlap within the three groups. People within the servicing group are themselves part of the work force. A significant number of people classified as *retired* actually work part-time. One person might find himself in all three groups: a pensioner under one system might find a second career in the pension-and-welfare field and begin to accumulate credits toward an additional pension payable on a second retirement from the work force.

To show the economic importance of private pensions, it is common to note the huge dollar values tied up in pension funds. A probable, unintended implication of this characterization is that pension funds are inactive funds. It is true that pension funds are not a source of venture capital, that is, pension funds are not used to *start* businesses. But irrespective of whether a fund is *trusteed* (and therefore usually administered by a professional investor such as a bank) or *insured* (and therefore invested by an insurance company), pension funds are invested in the productive capacity of the country through ownership of stocks, bonds, buildings, and land. Accumulated funds of private pension plans have grown enormously in the last forty years.[21] *Institutional investors* of private pension funds own about one-third of the total value of traded shares of stock of American companies. They provide *mortgage money* for innumerable construction projects, and they are constantly seeking outlets for funds.

The number of persons affected by pensions of all kinds and the sums of money involved make pensions a matter of political importance. For example, the matter of collective conscience aside, it is simply not

Introduction to Pensions 9

politically feasible to discontinue veterans pensions—since veterans and their families constitute a powerful political bloc. In addition, there are pension matters with political overtones that come to mind less readily. For example, are accumulated pension funds to be invested solely in accordance with the economic interest of the participants or, being public or quasi-public in nature, are they to be invested also in accordance with an overriding policy of government such as ending racial discrimination in South Africa, encouraging regional or local businesses, or encouraging some businesses over others to gain political advantage (for example, encouraging unionized rather than nonunionized businesses)?[22]

It is clear that government faces some obstacles in trying to guarantee to pension participants the disbursements to which they are entitled. Therefore, once government has insisted that investment of pension funds be free from corruption, conflict of interest, and speculation, it is at least arguable that government should refrain from entering further into the investment process. Nonetheless, turmoil in pension investment matters is foreseeable for years to come.

Criticisms of Pensions

Criticisms leveled at pension systems include the following: (1) Some are underfunded or unfunded (these are pay-as-you-go systems), and therefore offer little assurance of pension payments in the long run, although they are a source of pensions now. (2) Pensions originating in plans presupposing a stable currency prove inadequate when prices of goods and services rise. (3) In cases arising with noticeable frequency, pension systems (sometimes several in concert) pay pensions that exceed preretirement, earned income or that are inadequate. (4) Accumulated funds are used by bankers or insurers or other fund managers as a means of exercising inappropriate economic, social, or political power. (5) Many systems, such as social security, originate in a tax or a payroll deduction or a deferred wage that is involuntary; thus these systems are supported by some (for example, the independently wealthy) who might prefer not to support them at all. (6) Some systems are abused or corrupted.

All the forgoing criticisms are voiced from time to time. The intensity of the criticism and the interest with which it is received vary considerably and sometimes result in action. (For example, fears that the social security system is going bankrupt motivated Congress to raise the rate of the social security tax, or contribution, as it is euphemistically called.) A criticism less frequently voiced but of great impact both economically and socially is that the pension and health-care systems, considered in their entirety, are chaotic. They developed in a haphazard fashion, often for reasons that had little to do with any deepseated desire to afford a minimum competence to the retired and the disabled in the population. (Social security, for example, originated in part in efforts to remove older employees from the work force in order to reduce unemployment among the young.) The chaos did not result from design; but the result has been that the duplication, overlapping, and lack of integration of pension and health-care plans favor literate, informed people with the knowledge, interest, and time to maximize benefits from numerous sources. Although the time, effort, and money devoted to construing trusts and wills has been the cause of comment for decades, it is a little amount when compared to the time, effort, and money devoted to sorting out pension claims[23] and health-care benefits.

Conclusion

Pensions are part of the support (income-maintenance) system that has evolved in the United States over the last half-century. Through the support system the work force gives access to goods and services to the old, the retired, the disabled, the unemployed, the young, and the poor. The support system is based on the income-transfer (transfer payments) system by which those with higher incomes share with those of lower or no incomes. Existence of the support system presupposes a willingness by those in the work force to forgo some consumption themselves so that those drawing benefits from the support system might also have food, clothing, shelter, health care, and access to that part of our heritage owned in common, such as public parks and public museums.

Because the support system developed on a piecemeal basis and accommodated itself to social, political, and economic pressures, it works inefficiently,[24] quixotically, and at times unjustly. One part of the system often duplicates another part of the system, and some programs overlap. Nonetheless, whether support is in money or in kind or in a mix of the two, it is frequently inadequate and, paradoxically, occasionally excessive. The complexity of the system gives the edge in securing benefits to the educated, the well informed, the organized, and the aggressive with the time and patience required to establish eligibility and entitlement.

The pension system has not escaped the consequences of the erratic development of the support system of which pensions are a part. For example, in the 1970s Congress moved from ad hoc adjustment of social security benefits to an automatic adjustment of benefits that has proved to be troublesome. Questions on both the method and the adequacy of funding for social security have been raised. Abuse of the private-pension device led to the enactment of the Employee Retirement Income Security

Act of 1974 (ERISA) to assure to participants and beneficiaries their reasonable expectations from private pensions. The impact of ERISA, however, is limited. For example, ERISA does not mandate private pensions for those who have none, nor does it guaranty adequate retirement income to participants in private pension plans.

In the 1950s, 1960s, and 1970s, attention was directed to the rapid expansion of social security and to the proliferation and mismanagement of private pension plans. In the 1980s attention will be directed to the refinement of existing plans, to coordinating public and private pension plans, and to fitting pensions into the support system. To the extent that new private pension plans are created, they are likely to take the form of government-approved prototypes.[25] In short, the period of experimentation with pensions is probably over, and the period of maturity has set in.

This period of maturity begins in a time of inflation, sluggish capital formation, declining productivity, costly environmental protection, and significant demographic and family change. Just as most of us are becoming accustomed to having more, we find ourselves facing the distinct possibility of having less. If we have less, it is unrealistic to assume that the work force will bear a share of the disagreeable consequences of economic decline or stagnation that is greater than the share borne by the retired.

That being so, it is all the more important to try to modify the support system in such a way that it is socially, politically, and economically viable, for it simply cannot persist in the absence of a consensus among those working that it is worthwhile. Thus it is conventional to stress the elimination of fraud (or near fraud) in claiming benefits. But the principal flaw in the support system is not that it invites fraud. The principal flaw in the support system is that it is chaotic. Being chaotic, it all too frequently fails altogether, and it simply does not support those in need. And the support it does afford is needlessly expensive because of duplication and overlapping of programs and services.

It does not follow at all that in the name of efficiency we must abandon pluralism and diversity.[26] Although a support system created and administered solely by government might indeed work better than any other, that is not the kind of system that presently exists, and there is something to be said for diversity and variation. The United States is a large country, with regional and group aspirations and attitudes and numerous occupations. A support system geared to the needs of one region or one occupational group might prove unsuitable to another. The social security system uses age as a qualification for retirement benefits. A private-pension system might sensibly view years of service alone as sufficient qualification for retirement. (A coal miner below ground for thirty-five years can make a persuasive case for ready access to natural light for the rest of his life.)

We have engaged in extensive income redistribution for years, and we have finally created an income floor. It is true that frequently that income floor is inadequate, and sometimes it is unjustifiably withheld, but it was dearly won and ought not to be discarded lightly. To encourage the work force to retain the floor, we must try to assure that retirement or disability income (that is, replacement income, an element of the floor) does not exceed preretirement, earned income and that it does indeed permit the recipient to maintain a decent standard of living. It is not an easy task to provide that assurance, but we can provide it if we deeply desire to do so.

Pensions play a significant role as a source of retirement and disability income. Like the law on wills, trusts, and future interests, the law on pensions affects but a part of the population. But unlike the former, which is of interest principally to the wealthy, the latter is of interest to all economic groups. Even some from among the poor from time to time contribute to creation of pensions through *forfeitures* of interests that never vest. Just as improving the law on social security is clearly in the public interest in the largest sense, so too improving the law on private pensions is clearly in the interest of all segments of the population.

This process involves solving problems that have multiple aspects. For example, setting a ceiling on retirement or disability income is not only an economic matter but also a political and social matter. Fixing the elements of that ceiling might require *offsetting,* that is, reducing the amount of an element contributing to a beneficiary's income to preclude exceeding the ceiling. Offsetting calls for creation of legal formulas. Similarly, deciding whether accumulated pension funds should be invested to encourage location of industry within a city, state, or region not only has political and economic overtones but also raises legal questions. Encouraging the disabled and the elderly to remain in the work force to reduce pension costs entails changing conventional attitudes toward work and leaving the work force and requires assessing the price of retraining for new jobs, accommodating the workplace to the needs of the handicapped, and varying the length of the workday and the workweek. Assuring justice to the spouse of a participant in a pension plan must take into consideration the changing nature of the American family, the role of women in the work force, and our proclivity for turning difficult problems into constitutional law problems.

To make problems more manageable, we naturally try to define them as narrowly as possible. That tendency misleads us. If we are to work out long-run solutions to disability and retirement pension problems, we must look at the pension system as a part of the larger support system, and we must consider the political, economic, and social aspects of the system. By doing so, we can at least begin to reduce duplication and inefficiency and bring some order into an indefensibly chaotic state of affairs.

Notes

1. *The Guaranteed Income Proposal as Set Out in Free Men and Free Markets,* in The Guaranteed Income 227 (R. Theobald ed. 1966).
2. *See generally* D. Moynihan, The Politics of a Guaranteed Income 113–235 (1973).
3. 26 U.S.C. § 43 (Supp. 1982).
4. Some others are workers' compensation, supplemental security income, aid to families with dependent children, food stamps, and medicaid.
5. P. Drucker, The Unseen Revolution 1–46 (1976).
6. *See generally* Chapter 4 *infra,* Pensions in the Changing Wealth Transmission Process, at 65.
7. *See generally* Church, *A Debt-Threatened Dream,* Time, May 24, 1982, at 16.
8. The consumer price index is being reexamined. *See generally* Ehrbar, *How to Save Social Security,* Fortune, Aug. 25, 1980, at 34, 37; Fritz, *Is Consumer Price Index "Loaded"?,* U.S. News & World Report, Feb. 4, 1980, at 86.
9. *See generally* Glossary *infra,* at 165.
10. Banks are said to be losing pension-management business to competitors. *See generally* Saltzman, *It Takes More Than a Sincere Suit and a Smile,* Forbes, Apr. 16, 1979, at 116.
11. *See generally* Kemper, *Defined benefit H.R. 10 plans,* 66 A.B.A.J. 217 (1980).
12. *See generally* Alder, *Pension Programs under E.R.T.A. and Other Recent Developments,* 68 A.B.A.J. 358 (1982); *20 Questions— Answered—About IRAs,* Money, Apr. 1982, at 69.
13. *See generally* Scharff, *Planning Now for Retirement Later,* Money, July 1979, at 33; Main, *Building a 21st-Century Pension Right Now,* Money, Sept. 1976, at 38.
14. Keith, *Let's Throttle Back the Federal Pension Gravy Train,* The Reader's Digest, Sept. 1976, at 104.
15. Quinn, *Rating Pensions,* Newsweek, Feb. 12, 1979, at 76.
16. *See generally Will Inflation Tarnish Your Golden Years?,* U.S. News & World Report, Feb. 26, 1979, at 55.

17. A. Okun, Equality and Efficiency: The Big Tradeoff, 101–103 (1975).

18. *Why the Fuss over Retired Officers in Federal Jobs,* U.S. News & World Report, Feb. 7, 1977, at 39.

19. Social Security and Pensions: Programs of Equity and Security 16 (Staff Study, Joint Economic Committee, 96th Cong., 2d Sess., Oct. 1980).

20. *See generally* Chapter 3 *infra,* Pension Systems, at 41.

21. Assets total about $650 billion. Pension assets represent about 17 percent of all financial assets in the United States. Coming of Age: Toward a National Retirement Income Policy 18 (Final Report, President's Commission on Pension Policy, Feb. 26, 1981).

22. *See generally* Chapter 6 *infra,* Investing Pension Funds, at 111.

23. *Henry v. Goodwin,* 583 S.W.2d 29 (Ark. 1979) illustrates the interaction of the income-maintenance system and traditional property law. To qualify for supplemental security income, Alta Goodwin conveyed her home property of 87.29 acres to Lois Henry Thompson, a niece, with whom she had a "confidential relation," on the understanding that the grantee would thereafter reconvey to the grantor. The grantee died, and her heirs brought suit to quiet title. The Supreme Court of Arkansas found that under the circumstances a constructive trust arose in favor of Alta Goodwin and that she was not precluded by her conduct from asserting her interest in the property.

24. *See generally Service Industries: Growth Field of the '80s,* U.S. News & World Report, Mar. 17, 1980, at 80; *Capitol Hill's Growing Army of Bureaucrats,* U.S. News & World Report, Dec. 24, 1979, at 52; Bethell, *The Wealth of Washington,* Harper's, June 1978, at 41; *The Beneficent Monster,* Time, June 12, 1978, at 24.

25. *See generally* Cronin, *Keogh, Corporate, or I.R.A.: What's Best for You and Your Client,* 63 A.B.A.J. 1781 (1977).

26. E. Ginzberg, D. Hiestand, & B. Reubens, The Pluralistic Economy 1–32 (1965).

2

The Pension Crunch: The Population, the Work Force, and the Retired

In general, the work force in the United States supports those in the population who are not gainfully employed.[1] Traditionally, it did so directly—a husband supported his wife and children and sometimes his parents or other relatives; an unmarried adult child remained at home and supported his or her aged parents. To the extent that direct support was unavailable, dependent people without resources turned to charity or to very limited public-assistance programs of various kinds.

In nineteenth- and early-twentieth-century America, life for those in the work force tended to be hard and brief. Most of those able to work labored throughout life—only a fortunate few retired as old age approached. Income-maintenance difficulties for those in the work force originated in disability or in periodic unemployment resulting from economic distress or turmoil. When the head of the household had no income, his dependents suffered, and both he and his dependents turned to charity or sought public assistance.

Because the traditional support system simply failed in times of widespread economic distress, it was gradually supplanted by a public-support or income-maintenance system. In the 1930s some elements of the present support system appeared and achieved public acceptance, and in the ensuing forty years numerous other programs providing support payments in money or in kind were added.[2] Even prior to the 1930s some income-maintenance or income-replacement programs (veterans pensions, civil-service pensions, railroaders pensions, military pensions) existed, but they affected only a small part of the population and were not directed to relieving the effects of prolonged disability or unemployment on a large scale.

Today, workers' compensation, unemployment compensation, social security, federal and state civil-service pensions, military pensions, veterans pensions, railroaders pensions, supplemental security income, private pensions, medicare, medicaid, and numerous food, health, and housing programs provide support for the disabled, the unemployed, the retired, the old, the young, and the poor. So-called private pensions

---

Part of this chapter is drawn from R.J. Lynn, *Reducing Pension Costs Now: Three Suggestions,* 23 Ariz. L. Rev. 689 (1981). Copyright © by the Arizona Board of Regents. Reprinted by permission.

antedate the 1930s, but their spectacular growth paralleled the expansion of social security and closely related benefit plans in the period from 1940 to 1980.[3]

The federal income tax is a progressive tax. Those at the bottom of the income scale escape the tax entirely. The social security tax, or contribution, as it is styled, is a regressive tax. It must be paid by nearly everyone earning income, including those already retired and drawing social security benefits. The rate of the social security tax and the income base to which it applies have been increased in an effort to assure solvency of social security. Nonetheless, social security is in difficulties,[4] and the difficulties are unlikely to be solved by increases in the rate of tax and the tax base that are scheduled to take effect in the 1980s.

The benefits of the social security tax are enjoyed by beneficiaries of social security payments, principally the retired elderly and the retired disabled. The burden of the tax is borne by the work force, principally people whose ages range from the late teens through the middle sixties. Realistically, the social security system is a pay-as-you-go pension system. Those in the work force paying the social security tax are supporting those drawing social security benefits.[5]

Similarly, employees of governments and of private industry are participants in pension plans that require regular contributions to assure continuation of the plans. The contribution is made by the employee directly, through a payroll deduction, or indirectly, through payment made by the employer (a forgone wage). Some government pension plans are pay-as-you-go plans. Other government pension plans, like most private pension plans, are *funded* plans, that is, contributions are accumulated and invested. Irrespective of whether a plan is funded or unfunded, participants in government or private pension plans who are working are helping to support the retired beneficiaries of such plans. Some government[6] and private[7] pension plans are thought to be as unsound financially as social security. They may have promised more than they can deliver.

If the current work force supported only themselves and the retired elderly and the retired disabled, their burden would be a heavy one, for the retired have been increasing both in absolute numbers and as a proportion of the total population. But the work force also supports the unemployed, the young, the poor, and the disabled who have never entered the work force. When anyone who wishes to work finds ready employment, when wages are at least adequate (and sometimes generous), and the rate of inflation is so low that it passes unnoticed, the burden of support borne by the work force is tolerable. When the rate of unemployment is high and wages fail to keep pace with inflation, then the burden of support becomes heavy. If demographic changes add to the burden, at some point the burden becomes intolerable.

What underlies allusions to the *pension crunch*—the increasing burden of supporting the retired elderly and the retired disabled? What do we know about the American population, the nature of the work force, and the impact of dependency that leads us to think that changes in the age of retirement, the definition of disability, and the calculation of pension benefits are in order?

The Demographic Imperative

Generally speaking, people receiving support payments, including those receiving pensions, are consuming, not producing. Money and money equivalents in the form of goods and services that are channeled to pensioners are not being directed to investment and production. That being so, a case can easily be made for controlling pension costs because it is economically sensible to do so. Spending less on pensions permits greater spending on expanding and improving productive capacity.

However, the case for reducing pension costs does not rest solely on economic grounds. A realistic assessment of age groups within the population makes explicit the desirability of examining our pension systems now and restructuring and improving them before false expectations are raised and undesirable intergenerational conflict occurs.[8] There is reason to believe that the American work force willingly supports a reasonable number of nonworking people. However, accumulating evidence suggests that the American work force will not willingly support what it perceives to be an unreasonable number of nonworking people.[9]

Although *demography*—the study of the characteristics of human populations—is a comparatively new discipline, characteristics of particular populations have always been of interest to life insurers and pension planners. For example, the greater longevity of females as opposed to males is reflected by the mortality tables long used by insurers.[10] Now, as the proportion of older people in the population increases,[11] demography becomes a matter of interest to all and particularly to those in the work force supporting the old, the retired, the disabled, the unemployed, the young, and the poor.

What does the *population profile* look like now? How will it change before the turn of the century? Because information on population is gathered with regularity, we know a great deal about living Americans.[12]

We know also that the dramatic increase in the life span that resulted from improved diet, better sanitation, and the control of various insidious diseases probably is behind us, and we know that the decline in the birth rate that set in after the postwar "baby boom"[13] will result ultimately in a smaller proportion of persons within the population of childbearing age. But we do not know that a decline in the birthrate will continue, and we cannot be certain that a means of slowing the aging process will not be devised. Therefore, the population profile of the year 2000 is necessarily based in part on conjecture.

The population profile of the 1980s is not ideal, but that does not pose a threat to pension systems in the short run. The median age is slightly over thirty. Although the median age will rise gradually until well into the next century, nonetheless, there will be during the next several decades a proportionately large group within the working-age population that can support the nonworking population.

These comparatively numerous middle-aged people who finance and will continue to finance the support system will themselves age, and having been somewhat healthier than those in the generation preceding theirs, they will live just a little longer and will be somewhat more socially and politically active in later life than their parents were. Many in this age group have been beneficiaries of one or more segments of the support system from birth, and all in this age group naturally expect the support system to persist throughout life, including old age. To try without warning to withdraw part of the system—pensions, in particular—from this age group would create intergenerational bitterness and conflict not seen before in this country.

Yet some modification of support for the old is probable because the age group succeeding that which is now most numerous in the work force is a smaller generation, and therefore the burden of support will bear on that group comparatively more heavily. Although our population continues to grow, the proportion of the aged in the population grows faster.[14] There is sporadic grumbling now at what is perceived to be the privileged position of the pensioner. Unless a more rational and less chaotic system for supporting the nonworking (including the aged) is devised, the grumbling will become an insistent chorus.

Indeed, that clamor might be heard at a time much earlier than that conventionally predicted. Because those numerous persons born in the fifteen years after World War II will not retire in significant numbers until the next century is underway, and those born in the 1960s and 1970s who are then in the work force are from a smaller generation, the so-called pension crunch is frequently viewed as a matter that will not become critical until several decades have passed.

That view might prove to be illusory. There is a real possibility that an insistent demand for reducing the pension burden will be made during this decade. Those numerous persons born in the fifteen years after World War II have not found the job market as inviting as it was to the generation born in the 1930s and early 1940s who sought jobs in the 1950s and 1960s. Being exceptionally numerous, they must compete more vigorously with one another for entry-level jobs and promotions.[15] After successful entry into the labor force, advancement seems to be deferred for an unreasonable length of time. Moving up the ladder to better-paying jobs is the key to fulfilling expectations with respect to marriage, family, and lifestyle.[16] If the work force does not absorb this large generation in a way that its members think to be appropriate—if they think themselves to be relatively deprived—they are highly unlikely to forgo consumption themselves to support either the early retirement or the normal retirement of others who receive pensions that approach or exceed replacement income. Being numerous and having the vote, their voice will be heard on income-maintenance reform.

A pause here to consider a relevant question: Can pension reform (and reform of the income-maintenance system of which pensions are a part) be deferred or avoided altogether because of miscalculations? Will work and production in the future be so different from work and production now that the problem of income transfers (including pension costs) will be no problem at all?

Several decades ago it was suggested that automation would significantly transform the workplace. It was assumed that many employees would be idled, that relatively effortless production would result in an abundance of goods and services for distribution, and that an income base could be provided for all with little social and political friction.[17] Technology was to provide the key to social and political harmony.

Automation did affect the workplace. It idled some employees, and it unquestionably affected production. And there is a guaranteed income of sorts, consisting of a variety of money payments, payments in kind, and subsidies. But goods and services are not produced in such an abundance and at such low prices that allocation is not a problem. There are reasonable differences of opinion with respect to the emergence of a classless society in the United States. There can be no reasonable differences of opinion with respect to marked disparities in income that provides access to goods and services. Those at the top of the income scale are better housed, clothed, and fed than those at the bottom. Automation has made changes, but it has not created paradise.

Furthermore, expectations change. What is considered a luxury by most Americans today will not necessarily be considered a luxury twenty years hence. Such notions as "poverty level" and "income floor" are relative. And attitudes toward disparities in income will not necessarily be relatively tolerant. If the largest group within the work force finds itself precluded by sheer numbers alone from achieving the career advancement and concomitant income deemed its due, the income floor might be complemented by an income ceiling—that is, there might be an insistence on income leveling.

In short, experience with technological change suggests that there is only an outside chance of achieving that superabundance with minimal effort that will provide everyone with the good life. And even if superabundance based on current standards were to exist, rising expectations might transform it into abundance. More efficient production by robots is upon us,[18] but it is unlikely to prevent intergenerational and interclass dispute over cutting the pie.

The Population

Three factors affect total population and the population profile: fertility, mortality, and net immigration. The fertility rate measures the number of children an average woman bears in her lifetime. The birthrate measures the number of births within a designated group (for example, 1,000 Americans) for a designated time frame (for example, one year). The mortality rate measures the number of deaths within a designated group (for example, 1,000 Americans aged fifty-five or more) for a designated time frame (for example, one year). Net immigration is the difference between the number of aliens entering the United States and the number of people moving from the United States.

The effects of fertility and mortality on total population and the population profile cannot be predicted with certainty. If immigration into the United States were strictly controlled, the effect of net immigration could be predicted with considerable confidence. But immigration is not well controlled, and therefore the effect of net immigration also is uncertain.

Fertility

With the exception of the post-World War II period of the baby boom, the fertility rate in the United States has declined throughout this century. During the depression years it fell to the replacement rate of 2.1 children per woman.[19] (A fertility rate of 2.1 children per woman is considered necessary to maintain a stable population, for not all female children reach childbearing age.) During the baby boom the fertility rate rose to almost 3.8 births per woman, but it has since declined to a rate below the replacement rate. In the 1970s it was 1.8 births per woman.[20]

The reasons for the low fertility rate of the recent past are known to some extent. A principal contributing factor is the entry of women into the work force in significant numbers.[21] Irrespective of whether a woman enters the work force before or after bearing a child, her being at work affects her attitude toward childbearing. The age of marriage is being postponed by some women until their late twenties to permit qualifying for careers in the professions, and the years from age twenty to twenty-four are biologically the most fertile for women. Divorce is common, and the divorced woman is less likely to bear a child than the married woman. Other factors contributing to the decline in the fertility rate are awareness of contraception, improved methods of birth control, and the availability of legal abortions.[22]

Whether the low fertility rate of the 1970s will persist for an appreciable length of time is not known. It is possible that in time the workplace will accommodate women who bear children by providing generous maternity leaves and affording daycare facilities for preschool-aged children. Marriage as an institution might become more stable than it was during the 1960s and 1970s. Having three or four children rather than one or two might become attractive again. But if the fertility rate continues to be low, that will simply exacerbate foreseeable problems of providing adequate support in the next century to the numerous Americans born after World War II.

Even if the fertility rate remains low, the total population will continue to grow because there are now so many women alive capable of bearing children. It simply will not grow as fast as it would were the fertility rate to increase.

Mortality

Although Americans are living longer than ever before, the recent significant increase in the life span that we take for granted might not be repeated. In 1900 the average life expectancy was about forty-seven years; by 1930 it had risen to almost sixty.[23] Improvements in diet, sanitation, and medical technology that were made from 1900 to 1935 enabled Americans to avoid or overcome the killing diseases that once characterized childhood and middle age. Since the 1930s the average life span has increased to somewhat over seventy. Although there will be some reduction in the death rate during the next few decades, the reduction will most likely be only moderate.[24]

There are differences in life expectancy at birth between the sexes and between the races. By the mid-1970s, the difference in the life expectancy at birth of males and females was almost eight years.[25] The reasons for this difference are not clear. They may well include both environmental and biological factors. Whatever the causes, a consequence of the difference is more widows than widowers and a very high proportion of widows among the aged.

The difference in the life expectancy at birth of whites and nonwhites was five years in the mid-1970s, down from about eleven years in 1940.[26] Because the economic status of whites is better than that of blacks, environmental factors may play a greater role than biological factors in accounting for the difference.

The mortality rate of persons aged sixty-five or older began to fall in the late 1960s,[27] and the greatest increase in the life expectancy of persons aged seventy-five or older occurred in the period after 1965.[28] However, it is assumed that there will be no dramatic reduction in the death rate in the decades ahead.

Net Immigration

Since 1978 legal immigration into the United States has been limited to a worldwide figure of 290,000 persons. Those exempt from the legal limitation include parents, spouses, and children of U.S. citizens, and various classes of special immigrants, including political refugees.[29]

During the years 1967 to 1978, legal immigrants numbering 4.3 million entered at the rate of about 400,000 a year.[30] They accounted for some 20 percent of population growth.[31] About the same number of illegal immigrants probably entered during the same period.[32] In 1978, 601,000 entered legally.[33] The 1980 Cuban and Haitian refugees swelled the number to more than 800,000.[34]

During the decade of peak immigration between 1900 and 1910,[35] about 8.8 million immigrants entered the United States. The figure resulting from the combination of legal and illegal immigration of the late 1960s and the 1970s probably surpasses the figure from the earlier peak period. Because figures on illegal immigration are estimates,[36] the total number of aliens who have entered the United States during the last twenty years is not known. Officials estimate that nearly 6 million illegal aliens are now residing here.[37]

Total Population, the Dependent Population, and the Work Force

The United States has a population of about 229 million,[38] and the population continues to grow, although at a rate slower than that prevailing after World War II. Females outnumber males by about 6 million.[39] Whites constitute about 86 percent of the population; blacks, about 12 percent.[40] During the 1970s the number of blacks increased at a rate one and one-half times the rate of the rest of the population, and the number of Hispanics increased at an even faster rate.[41]

Although the population is growing, it is also aging. The number of children aged fourteen and younger decreased by 11.5 percent in the 1970s while the number of people aged sixty-five or older increased by 28 percent.[42] The median age is slightly over thirty. (About half of the total population is over thirty, and about half is under thirty.) By the year 2000 the median age will rise gradually to nearly thirty-five.[43]

As the two preceding paragraphs indicate, segments of the population are identified by such characteristics as sex, race, and age (female, black, the elderly). The support or income-maintenance system evolved by identifying segments of the population with a widely shared characteristic (for example, poverty or unemployment). Some population characteristics (for example, employability and dependency) are of particular interest in assessing the viability of the support system because they affect viability directly. Some characteristics (for example, level of education and geographical location) bear less directly on viability. Because dependent persons often fall under more than one characteristic (for example, both poverty and unemployment), they frequently qualify for benefits under more than one support program. The result is overlapping programs, with consequent confusion, ill-will, waste, and occasional fraud. The following discussion will identify first the principal population groups that fall within the support system; thereafter, the composition and characteristics of the work force will be discussed.

The Elderly. A highly visible group in the population consists of those people aged sixty-five or older, usually called the *elderly* or the *aged*. Some investigators break the elderly into two groups, the *young-old* (aged sixty-five to eighty) and the *old-old* (aged eighty or more). Now numbering about 25 million, the number of elderly is growing at a rate about twice that of the general population. The elderly in the United States outnumber the entire population of Canada.[44] By the year 2000 they will number nearly 32 million.[45]

In the first third of this century, the number of elderly men about equalled the number of elderly women. Today both men and women are living longer than they did at the turn of the century, and they live about three years longer after age sixty-five than they did at the inception of social security.[46] But the life expectancy of women has outstripped that of men. There are about two men aged sixty-five or older for every three women in that age group.[47]

Contrary to common belief, older people usually maintain separate households.[48] Seventy percent own their own homes.[49] Only about 10 percent of those aged sixty-five or older are institutionalized or are cared for at home.[50] But the longer the elderly live, the greater the sums that are paid to them in retirement benefits, and the greater the likelihood that they will need expensive medical care. Support programs for the elderly account for about one-fourth of the entire federal budget.

Veterans. Among the aging are the veterans of World War II. Of the 30 million American veterans, 12.4 million served during the years 1941 to 1945. Their average age is sixty-one.[51] By 1985 a majority of them will be sixty-five; many will be retired and will be much more likely than veterans under age sixty-five to require health care. During the 1970s the annual budget of the Veterans' Administration (VA) (expended principally for pensions and health care) more than doubled. It is now in the $25 billion to $30 billion range. Each month the VA mails over $1 billion in checks to recipients of veterans benefits—veterans, their dependents, and survivors.[52]

The Young. Because the fertility rate declined during the 1960s and 1970s, there are proportionately fewer children in the population now than there were in the years after World War II. The number of children in public elementary and secondary schools declined from approximately 45.6 million in 1970 to approximately 42.6 million in 1979.[53] In Catholic schools the decline for the period was from approximately 9.4 million to 8.1 million.[54] In the 1970s communities closed some grade schools; in the 1980s they will close some high schools. However, if the numerous women now of childbearing age decide to have three or four children rather than one or two, elementary schools quickly would fill again.

Most children are supported by their working parent or parents. Some are supported through a great range of children's support services, including the federally funded aid to families with dependent children (AFDC), with an annual budget exceeding seven billion dollars. Among children supported by AFDC are many illegitimates. The number of illegitimate births increased in the United States throughout the 1970s. There were nearly 600,000 in 1979, an increase of 10 percent over 1978.[55] One out of every six babies is an illegitimate. Many illegitimates are born to teenagers. Nearly a third of babies born to white teenagers are illegitimate; over three-fourths of those born to black teenagers are illegitimate. Unmarried teenage mothers are unlikely to support their children, and the burden of supporting the illegitimate children of teenagers falls on the work force.

The Disabled. Neither physical nor mental disability is confined to any single age group in the population (although both are visited regularly on the very old). Handicapped people are found throughout the population, irrespective of age, race, or sex. The number of handicapped Americans turns on the definition of handicap. One estimate puts the number as high as 50 million—an estimate surely on the high side.[56] Because disability from military service is confined to identified people, it is known that there are about 3.5 million disabled American veterans, half of whom are veterans of World War II.[57]

Not every disability precludes joining the work force. Many handicapped people are employed. But some 10 or 20 million mentally normal people have serious physical, sensory, or health-related handicaps.[58] Some people suffer from severe mental illness. It follows that some of the handicapped are so severely disabled that they are unemployable. Some who might work are denied employment even in periods of peak employment. The disabled are supported by a wide range of programs including workers' compensation, social security, supplemental security income (SSI), and veterans pensions.

The Unemployed. The number of Americans who are working has increased fairly steadily since World War II. Between 1973 and 1978, 10 million people entered the work force.[59] Most were young adults; many were women. In 1970 there were about 8 million male workers aged eighteen to twenty-four in the civilian work force; in 1980 there were more than 11 million.[60]

Nonetheless, there are millions of Americans unemployed and seeking work. Toward the end of the 1960s, the unemployment rate was less than 4 percent.[61] From 1970 to 1977 it averaged 6.25 percent.[62] Moving further into the decade of the 1980s, the unemployment rate hovers at the 10-percent figure, lower in some areas (the South and the West), much higher in the areas of heavy industry (the upper Midwest). Because there are many more whites than blacks, the unemployed are more often white than black, but the percentage of unemployed blacks is much higher than that of whites.

The high rate of unemployment now as compared to that of the late 1960s is attributable to a combination of circumstances: the coming of age of the baby-boom generation, the entry of women into the work force at an accelerating rate, the inability of American industry to compete effectively with foreign industry, and our withdrawal in the 1970s from the war economy of the 1960s. Some of these factors will not change quickly.

Whatever the causes of unemployment, the costs are borne ultimately by the work force. An increase of 1 percent in the unemployment rate costs $25 billion in lost taxes and unemployment benefits.[63] Nearly all workers are eligible for unemployment compensation under qualifications and in amounts that vary from state to state,[64] but most benefits end when a worker has been unemployed for nine months.[65] Only about half the unemployed are drawing benefits.[66]

The Poor. The level at which income is so low that an American is living in poverty is a matter on which there is no agreement. If income insufficient to keep a family above the *poverty level* results in poverty, then it is agreed that the proportion of Americans living in poverty is lower than it was in 1960. Many households have been lifted from poverty by the remarkable increase in the number and scope of income-transfer (or transfer-payments) programs initiated or expanded by the federal government after the Great Society of the Johnson administration was launched in the 1960s. Identifiable segments of the population chronically afflicted by low incomes or no incomes at all—the aged, the severely handicapped, mothers with small children and no wage earner—benefit from incomes, income supplements, and in-kind benefits created by law. Among them are supplemental security income (SSI), aid to families with dependent children (AFDC), food stamps, medicaid, and various kinds of subsidized housing.

About 4.2 million needy aged, blind, and disabled people are beneficiaries of supplemental security income costing $8 billion annually.[67] About 21.5 million people (one of every ten people in the population) in about 8 million households[68] receive food stamps costing $9.6 billion annually. The number of people receiving food stamps has nearly doubled since 1972.[69] About one-third of all households receiving food stamps have one or more people receiving supplemental security income or social security benefits.[70] About 23 million people are beneficiaries of medicaid, a health-care program funded by both federal and state governments. The federal share costs more than $17 billion.[71]

The Work Force. More than 100 million people—nearly half the population—are working.[72] Those in private, nonagricultural employment have incomes averaging $13,000 a year.[73] Those employed by government earn somewhat more;[74] those in agricultural employment markedly less. Although regional differences in incomes are narrowing,[75] there are great disparities in earned incomes in all parts of the United States and regrettable differences in the incomes of groups: The median income of black families is only 59 percent of that of white families;[76] women earn only 60 cents for every dollar that men earn.[77]

A majority of employed Americans are now classified as *white-collar* workers. The upsurge in white-collar work is attributable principally to greatly increased numbers of people in *services* (health care, insurance, banking, finance, government, transportation, and hotel and restaurant work). *Blue-collar* employment is a proportionately less significant part of total employment than it was at the close of World War II, and its relative significance continues to decline.[78] Although both agriculture and manufacturing are essential to the economic health of the nation, each engages proportionately fewer workers each year. The number of people in agriculture and related employment remained at about 3.5 million throughout the 1970s.[79] The number of people working in manufacturing (22 million) is about the same as the number working in wholesale and retail trade.[80]

The most numerous group in the work force consists of people born in the fifteen years after World War II, 1946 to 1961, the years of the baby boom when 64 million children were born.[81] Frequently these persons are considered a *generation* or a *cohort*. They crowded elementary schools, high schools, and colleges in the 1950s and 1960s. Now in their midtwenties to midthirties, they too will age, and by 1990 they will be regarded as middle-aged. They began entering the work force in large numbers in the late 1960s. Those under age thirty-five accounted for 96 percent of the net growth of the work force during the 1968 to 1973 period.[82] The baby-boom generation accounts for a high proportion of new households and consumes a high proportion of the durable goods that households acquire. Because the number of people in the baby-boom generation is so great as compared to the numbers of people in the generations preceding and following them, the baby-boom generation creates a bulge in the population that will persist into the next century. That bulge is the cause of an undesirable *dependency ratio* that will deeply affect the structure of the support system of the future.

Half the children born during the baby-boom years were female, and many of them are now in the work force. Of every hundred workers, about forty are women. About half of all adult women are employed,[83] and about 60 percent of women under age thirty-five are employed.[84] Some working women never have married. Some are married and work because they prefer to be occupied outside the home. Many married women work because they must; meeting household expenses requires two incomes. Numerous working women are separated or divorced. One of every seven families is headed by a woman.[85] The disarray of the American family does not account entirely for the great influx of women into the work force, but it contributes to it.

Most working women are not well paid. During the 1970s when women were entering the work force at an accelerating rate, services and retail trade provided more than 70 percent of all new jobs in the private sector.[86] Wages in services and retail trade are markedly lower than those in manufacturing (employees in health-care facilities earned an average of $3.87 per hour in 1979; employees in manufacturing, $6.69).[87] Furthermore, many jobs in services and retail trade offer little opportunity for advancement. In banking, women hold 80 percent of the clerical jobs and less than 20 percent of the managerial jobs.[88] So-called female jobs (for example, nursing and elementary school teaching) still are dominated by women.[89] Women are a significant part of the work force, but they are typically in low-paying, dead-end jobs.

At the start of the 1970s, the *work-force-participation rates* (the number employed compared to the number of working age) of white males and black males were nearly the same. However, black males did not share proportionately in the remarkable gains in employment that occurred during the 1970s, and, similarly, minority women increased their work-force participation only modestly. The employment gains that blacks have made tend to be in the service and trade sectors of the economy where wages are low.[90] Just as women as a group earn less than men, so too blacks as a group earn less than whites.

Immigrants, including perhaps as many as 6 million illegal aliens, are an essential part of the economy—they do much of the menial work in agriculture, the garment industry, and hotels and restaurants.[91] Illegals may constitute as much as 30 percent of the low-skilled work force.[92] Although immigrants start at the bottom of the pay scale, they advance where opportunity permits. One study revealed that after five years in the United States, earnings of legally admitted, foreign-born Americans were 9.5 percent lower than those of natives; after thirty years, earnings were 13 percent higher than those of natives.[93]

About 44 million Americans are middle aged—aged forty-five to sixty-four. Younger men in this age group are usually in the work force, and a significant number of women workers are drawn from this group including some who have raised families, gone back to school, and reentered the work force after a long absence. Professional, executive, and managerial positions tend to be held by men who are middle aged, and drawn from the age forty-five to sixty-four group.[94]

About 38 million Americans are fifty-five or older.[95] People withdrawing from the work force because of disability are drawn from all age groups, for accident and ill health are no respecters of youth. Those withdrawing because of age are usually in their fifties and beyond. Little more than a generation ago nearly half of all men sixty-five or older were still in the work force. Today only one man in five in that age group is working or seeking work, and among older women, only one in twelve.[96] Older Americans in their sixties and beyond are usually out of the work force, and most of them are heavily dependent on the support system.

Productivity, the Economy, and the Dependency Ratio

The willingness of the work force to support the dependent population turns in part on the ready availability of goods and services in quantities sufficient to satisfy the needs of all. The availability of goods and services is a consequence of productivity. Productivity measures efficiency in the use of labor, capital, and natural resources. Usually productivity is expressed as a relationship (ratio) between goods and services *(output)* and labor, capital, and natural resources *(input)*.[97] The higher the rate of productivity, the greater the quantity of goods and services available for distribution. An increase in the rate has the same effect. A decline in the rate of productivity (or a deceleration of an increasing rate) usually is regarded as undesirable and portentous.

The period from the end of World War II to the mid-1960s was a time of unparalleled prosperity in the United States, and it was characterized by a growth of productivity. Since the mid-1960s, productivity growth has declined.[98] Among the reasons cited for the decline are: (1) the entry into the labor force of large numbers of inexperienced young and female workers, (2) the aging and obsolescence of plants and equipment, (3) the propensity for spending rather than saving, (4) the shift from manufacturing to services, (5) environmental regulations, (6) unexpected high increases in the costs of energy, (7) inflation, (8) decreasing emphasis on research and development, (9) ineffective management, and (10) attitudes toward work.

While productivity growth was declining, the United States was also losing its competitive edge in world markets. For years the United States was the leading exporter of manufactured goods. West Germany has overtaken the United States in that respect, and Japan is close to doing so.[99] Although the United States still has the strongest economy of the industrialized nations,[100] the economy has lost its momentum.[101]

Is the decline in productivity growth irreversible? Is the slowing of the American economy permanent? Is it unrealistic to assume a slow but steady rise in the standard of living in the United States? In particular, should the dependent segments of the population lower their expectations of receiving a fairer share of the goods and services available for distribution from time to time?

There is simply no agreement on what the future holds for the American economy. Some suggest that this is an age of decline,[102] and not all who perceive the decline think it to be unfortunate. If society has become too materialistic, too much preoccupied with raising personal incomes and increasing possessions, it has been suggested that in the long run it may be in society's best interest to cultivate a simpler life, a life less dependent on material progress. Some think that the idea of progress—

an idea that unquestionably has pervaded American life since the founding of the republic—is itself in jeopardy.[103]

But not all are pessimistic. Just as the reasons assigned for the decline in productivity are numerous, the suggestions for improving productivity are multiple[104]: (1) increase the supply of capital available for modernizing plants and equipment, (2) increase expenditures for research and development, (3) improve management, (4) improve communication with and motivation of employees, (5) eliminate or modify federal regulations that unjustifiably inhibit productivity, (6) adopt monetary and fiscal policies that check inflation, (7) improve the infrastructure of the nation (roads, rail systems, water and sewage systems, waterways), and (8) reduce crime.

There is no doubt that Americans save proportionately less than their counterparts in West Germany and Japan, and it is equally clear that expenditures in the United States for research and development, on the one hand, and for plant and equipment, on the other, have fallen off.[105] The estimated average age of plant and equipment is sixteen to seventeen years in the United States, twelve years in West Germany, and ten years in Japan.[106] It is said that management has been preoccupied with maximizing short-term profits and has failed to take the long view.[107] Whether productivity has declined because American workers are lazier than they once were is debatable,[108] but there is accumulating evidence that a higher proportion of Americans than ever before seek work that is satisfying.[109]

If an expanding economy and improved productivity are the keys to maintaining an improved standard of living for all, both the work force and the retired have a stake in the reindustrialization of the country. The dependency ratio in itself makes that clear. There are now five people of working age for each person sixty-five or older.[110] By the third decade of the next century there might be only three people of working age for each person sixty-five or older. The burden of support borne by the work force is already heavy. Population figures and projections indicate that the burden surely will increase.

Conclusion

Pension benefits are but one element of a disorderly, inefficient income-maintenance system that developed over several decades. Because pensions are just a part of the income-maintenance system, pensioners compete with other beneficiaries of the support system—the unemployed, the young, the poor, and the disabled—for those goods and services allocated to the dependent population by the work force. Ready availability of goods and services turns on the number of persons at work, the rate of productivity, and the state of the economy. A busy, productive work force is likely to provide the dependent with a decent standard of living. A work force beset by unexpected layoffs, so-called stagflation, and falling expectations is likely to take care of itself before it extends generosity to others.

The great number of retired elderly in the U.S. population is a phenomenon of the last half of the twentieth century that becomes more evident, and more troublesome, with every passing year. People aged sixty-five or more now constitute about 11 percent of the population, and the percentage is expected to rise steadily for several decades.[111] It is to the credit of Americans that they have extended benefits to the elderly, but it is not to their credit that benefits have been periodically increased without taking account of the proportionately larger number of older people in the population as compared to those in the work force who bear the burden of the support system. And it is not to their credit that the foreseeable problem of providing support payments at adequate levels in years of economic difficulties has been ignored.

Pensions depend on a number of factors: first, an implicit promise by those at work to support the retired in return for assurance that those now at work in turn will be supported when a time for support arises; second, a healthy economy that produces goods and services in quantities sufficient to satisfy the needs of those at work and those not working; and third, an efficient system of providing benefits to the dependent segments of the population.

In the years after World War II, the United States committed itself to creating an income-maintenance system, and that commitment still stands. If the commitment is to be honored, we must take into account the nature of the population and its expectations, the necessity for revitalizing the economy and rebuilding or repairing the infrastructure of the nation, and the possibility of producing goods and services in adequate quantities despite an unfavorable dependency ratio.

Revitalizing the economy and rebuilding or repairing the infrastructure of the nation require vast capital expenditures.[112] The United States is a rich country. Despite decades of exploitation, it is still rich in natural resources, and it has a large working-age population. But does it have a deep desire to raise the capital needed to regain industrial and commercial preeminence in the world? Will it forgo consumption to provide the means to rebuild?

Pensions are a part of the income-transfer system by which those in the work force support the dependent population. Successful pension systems require a regular flow of funds from those at work. The greater the number of people at work as compared to those not working and the greater the rate of productivity, the less the financial strain on pension systems.

The favorable dependency ratio that has existed in the United States will become less favorable. If the standard of living (including that of pensioners) that exists in the United States is to be maintained, we must (1) raise capital to invest in productive capacity and to rebuild or repair the infrastructure; (2) get as many working-age people as possible into the work force and keep them there; and (3) improve productivity. Nothing less will do. The pension crunch is already upon us.

Notes

1. If an employee or a self-employed person forgoes consumption to save from earned income in the traditional way, and on becoming unemployed, disabled, or old draws on savings for replacement income, he is not dependent on the work force for replacement income. Such saving occurs, but it is not the principal source of replacement income, and it has not been for several decades. Contributions to pension plans are the savings from which some disability or retirement incomes are paid, but generally speaking, pension plans are part of the income-transfer (or transfer-payments) system. There is great disparity in earned incomes in the United States. People with high incomes can, if they wish, save in the traditional way. Some people have incomes high enough to permit saving, but they do not choose to save. Others have incomes so low that they cannot save. The inequities of the earned-income structure underlie the income-maintenance system of which pensions are a part, but the inequities are beyond the scope of this book.

2. B. Stein, Social Security and Pensions in Transition 38–60 (1980).

3. D. McGill, Fundamentals of Private Pensions 16–28 (3d ed. 1975).

4. *See generally* Church, *A Debt-Threatened Dream,* Time, May 24, 1982, at 16.

5. In the 1960s the *dependency ratio*—those in the work force compared to those drawing social security—was five to one; by the year 2035, the ratio will be two to one. Beck, *The Baby Boomers Come of Age,* Newsweek, Mar. 30, 1981, at 34, 37.

6. Funding of State and Local Government Pension Plans: A Na-

tional Problem iv (Report to the Congress by the Comptroller General of the United States, Aug. 30, 1979).

7. Ehrbar, *Those Pension Plans Are Even Weaker Than You Think*, Fortune, Nov. 1977, at 104.

8. S. Ross, Income Security Programs: Past, Present and Future 51–58 (Working Paper for the President's Commission on Pension Policy, Oct. 1980).

9. Quinn, *The Affluent Elders,* Newsweek, Aug. 4, 1980, at 53.

10. In *City of Los Angeles, Department of Power and Water v. Manhart,* 435 U.S. 702 (1978), the Supreme Court held that under Title VII of the Civil Rights Act of 1964 and the Equal Pay Act of 1963, it is unlawful to require female employees to make larger pension-fund contributions than those required of male employees in order to receive the same monthly benefit on retirement. Abandonment of sex-based actuarial tables has run into difficulties. Fields, *TIAA-CREF to Defer 'Unisex' Pensions until Court Resolves 2 Lawsuits,* The Chronicle of Higher Education, May 12, 1982, at 1, cols. 2–4; Fields, *Equal Pension Benefits Ordered for Men and Women,* The Chronicle of Higher Education, Mar. 31, 1982, at 1, cols. 2–4.

11. By the year 2020, the number of people aged sixty-five and over will about double. Siegel, *Recent and Prospective Demographic Trends for the Elderly Population and Some Implications for Health Care,* in Second Conference on the Epidemiology of Aging 289 [U.S. Department of Health and Human Services Publication No. (NIH) 80–969, July 1980].

12. *See generally* Human Resources & Demographics: Characteristics of People and Policy 9–37 (Staff Study, Joint Economic Committee, 96th Cong., 2d Sess., Nov. 1980).

13. The most significant group in the working population in the decades ahead consists of those born in the years from 1946 to 1961— about 64 million. The youngest in this group will reach normal retirement age in the third decade of the next century. *See generally* Guzzardi, *Demography's Good News for the Eighties,* Fortune, Nov. 1979, at 92.

14. *See generally,* Mayer, *The Graying of America,* Newsweek, Feb. 28, 1977, at 50.

15. P. Blumberg, Inequality in an Age of Decline 48–50 (1980); R. Easterlin, Birth and Fortune 19–32 (1980).

16. *See generally* Kiechel, *Two-Income Families Will Reshape the Consumer Markets,* Fortune, Mar. 10, 1980, at 110.

17. *See The Guaranteed Income Proposal as Set Out in Free Men and Free Markets,* in The Guaranteed Income 227–233 (R. Theobald ed. 1966).

18. *See generally* Main, *Work Won't Be the Same Again,* Fortune,

June 28, 1982, at 58; Friedrich, *The Robot Revolution,* Time, Dec. 8, 1980, at 72.

19. B. Torrey, Demographic Shifts and Projections, the Implications for Pensions 2 (Working Paper for the President's Commission on Pension Policy, Apr. 1979).

20. Human Resources & Demographics: Characteristics of People and Policy 9 (Staff Study, Joint Economic Committee, 96th Cong., 2d Sess., Nov. 1980).

21. *Id.* 10.

22. B. Torrey, Demographic Shifts and Projections, The Implications for Pensions 6 (Working Paper for the President's Commission on Pension Policy, Apr. 1979).

23. *Id.* 9.

24. Siegel, *Recent and Prospective Demographic Trends for the Elderly Population and Some Implications for Health Care,* in Second Conference on the Epidemiology of Aging 289, 307 [U.S. Department of Health and Human Services Publication No. (NIH) 80–969, July 1980].

25. *Id.* 301.

26. *Id.* 304.

27. *Id.* 299.

28. B. Torrey, Demographic Shifts and Projections, the Implications for Pensions 10 (Working Paper for the President's Commission on Pension Policy, Apr. 1979).

29. U.S. Department of Commerce, Bureau of the Census, Statistical Abstract of the United States 90 (1980).

30. Berman, *Does the Melting Pot Still Meld?* Forbes, Oct. 30, 1978, at 63, 65.

31. Guzzardi, *Demography's Good News for the Eighties,* Fortune, Nov. 5, 1979, at 92, 98.

32. Berman, *Does the Melting Pot Still Meld?* Forbes, Oct. 30, 1978, at 63.

33. U.S. Department of Commerce, Bureau of the Census, Statistical Abstract of the United States 91 (1980).

34. *Controls for an Alien Invasion,* Time, Aug. 3, 1981, at 17.

35. Hauser, *The Population of the United States, Retrospect and Prospect,* in The Population Dilemma 86 (P. Hauser ed. 2d ed. 1963).

36. Wachter, *Second Thoughts about Illegal Immigrants,* Fortune, May 22, 1978, at 80.

37. Alexander, Branegan, & Melvoin, *Notes from the Underground,* Time, Sept. 7, 1981, at 54.

38. U.S. Department of Commerce, Bureau of the Census, Sup-

plementary Report, Provisional Estimates of Social, Economic, and Housing Characteristics 3 (Mar. 1982); *Latest Profile of America's People,* U.S. News & World Report, Sept. 14, 1981, at 26, 27.

39. *Profile of America,* U.S. News & World Report, Apr. 7, 1980, at 64.

40. *How Population Shifts Are Changing America,* U.S. News & World Report, Mar. 5, 1979, at 76, 77.

41. *Latest Profile of American People,* U.S. News & World Report, Sept. 14, 1981, at 26, 29.

42. *Id.* 28.

43. Mayer, *The Graying of America,* Newsweek, Feb. 28, 1977, at 50, 52.

44. Little, *Changing Demographic Patterns and Some Potential Implications for Nonmetropolitan America,* in Human Resources and Demographics: Characteristics of People and Policy, Joint Economic Committee, 96th Cong., 2d Sess., 153, 158 (Dec. 1980).

45. Diggs, *Baby Boomlet: Its Impact on the '80s,* U.S. News & World Report, June 15, 1981, at 51, 52.

46. B. Torrey, Demographic Shifts and Projections, The Implications for Pension Systems 20 (Working Paper for the President's Commission on Pension Policy, Apr. 1979).

47. *Id.* 22.

48. Neugarten, *Growing Old in 2020: How Will It Be Different?* 61 Nat. Forum, Phi Kappa Phi J. 28, 29 (1981).

49. *Life Begins at 55,* U.S. News & World Report, Sept. 1, 1980, at 50, 56.

50. *The Happiest Americans—Who Are They?* U.S. News & World Report, Dec. 24, 1979, at 64, 66.

51. Starr & Hager, *VA Benefits: Running Out?,* Newsweek, Nov. 9, 1981, at 49.

52. Feinsilber, *Criticized VA Now 50,* Columbus (Oh.) Dispatch, Aug. 3, 1980, p. E12, col. 3.

53. U.S. Department of Commerce, Bureau of the Census, Statistical Abstract of the United States 154 (1980).

54. *Id.* 155.

55. *Black and White, Unwed All Over,* Time, Nov. 9, 1981, at 67.

56. Featherstone, review of S. Kleinfield, The Hidden Minority: America's Handicapped, The New Republic, Feb. 2, 1980, at 30.

57. *Id.*

58. Gliedman & Roth, *The Unexpected Minority,* The New Republic, Feb. 2, 1980, at 26.

59. Wernick & McIntire, *Employment and Labor Force Growth: Recent Trends and Future Prospects,* in Human Resources and Demographics, Joint Economic Committee, 96th Cong., 2d Sess., 101 (Dec. 1980).

60. *End of Youth Boom, Meaning for the Nation,* U.S. News & World Report, Nov. 9, 1981, at 66, 67.

61. Byron, *The Idle Army of Unemployed,* Time, Aug. 11, 1980, at 44, 45.

62. Wachter, *Second Thoughts about Illegal Immigrants,* Fortune, May 22, 1978, at 80, 81.

63. Byron, *The Idle Army of Unemployed,* Time, Aug. 11, 1980, at 44, 45.

64. Failey & Thornton, *The Great Ripoff in Unemployment Pay,* U.S. News & World Report, Mar. 16, 1981, at 63, 64.

65. Kelly, *Unemployment on the Rise,* Time, Feb. 8, 1982, at 22, 24.

66. Byron, *The Idle Army of Unemployed,* Time, Aug. 11, 1980, at 44, 45.

67. *Federal Benefits for People: $1 Out of $2,* U.S. News & World Report, May 18, 1981, at 54, 55.

68. *Facts about Food Stamps,* CNI Weekly Report, Mar. 5, 1981, at 4.

69. *Federal Benefits for People: $1 Out of $2,* U.S. News & World Report, May 18, 1981, at 54, 55.

70. *Facts about Food Stamps,* CNI Weekly Report, Mar. 5, 1981, at 4.

71. *Federal Benefits for People: $1 Out of $2,* U.S. News & World Report, May 18, 1981, at 54, 55.

72. U.S. Department of Commerce, Bureau of the Census, Supplementary Report, Provisional Estimates of Social, Economic, and Housing Characteristics 25 (Mar. 1982); *Can Reagan Rekindle Long-Term Growth?,* U.S. News & World Report, Oct. 26, 1981, at 42.

73. *Who's Ahead, Who's Behind in Real Pay,* U.S. News and World Report, May 18, 1981, at 93.

74. *Federal Workers Brace to Fend Off Reagan,* U.S. News & World Report, Feb. 23, 1981, at 79, 80.

75. *States Where Incomes Will Rise Fastest,* U.S. News & World Report, Dec. 22, 1980, at 50.

76. *Profile of America,* U.S. News & World Report, Apr. 7, 1980, at 64, 66.

77. *Breakthrough in the Wage War,* Time, June 22, 1981, at 70.

78. Wernick & McIntire, *Employment and Labor Force Growth: Recent Trends and Future Prospects* in Human Resources and Demo-

graphics: Characteristics of People and Policy, Joint Economic Committee, 96th Cong., 2d Sess., 101 (Dec. 1980).

79. U.S. Department of Commerce, Bureau of the Census, Statistical Abstract of the United States 406 (1980).

80. *The Leap toward a Service Society,* U.S. News & World Report, Oct. 12, 1981, at 66.

81. Beck, *The Baby Boomers Come of Age,* Newsweek, Mar. 30, 1981, at 34.

82. Wernick & McIntire, *Employment and Labor Force Growth: Recent Trends and Future Prospects,* in Human Resources and Demographics, Joint Economic Committee, 96th Cong., 2d Sess., 101, 111 (Dec. 1980).

83. *Id.* 103.

84. *Id.* 113.

85. *Working Women, Joys and Sorrows,* U.S. News & World Report, Jan. 15, 1979, at 64. Most of these families are poor. *See generally* Moynihan, *One-third of a Nation,* The New Republic, June 9, 1982, at 18; Harrington, *The Lower Depths,* The New Republic, June 9, 1982, at 26, 27.

86. Rothschild, *Reagan and the Real America,* The New York Review of Books, Feb. 5, 1981, at 12.

87. *Id.* 13.

88. *Working Women, Joys and Sorrows,* U.S. News & World Report, Jan 15, 1979, at 64, 65.

89. *Battle of the Sexes, Men Fight Back,* U.S. News & World Report, Dec. 8, 1980, at 50, 51.

90. Wernick & McIntire, *Employment and Labor Force Growth: Recent Trends and Future Prospects,* in Human Resources and Demographics, Joint Economic Committee, 96th Cong., 2d Sess., 101, 116, 121, 126 (Dec. 1980).

91. Alexander, *Notes from the Underground,* Time, Sept. 7, 1981, at 54.

92. Wachter, *Second Thoughts about Illegal Immigrants,* Fortune, May 22, 1978, at 80, 81.

93. Berman, *Does the Melting Pot Still Meld,* Forbes, Oct. 30, 1978, at 63, 65.

94. *Latest Findings on Middle-Age Americans,* U.S. News & World Report, Aug. 3, 1981, at 41.

95. *Life Begins at 55,* U.S. News & World Report, Sept. 1, 1980, at 50.

96. Shabecoff, *A Fast-Aging Population,* The New York Times, July 29, 1978, Section III, p. 16, reprinted in J. Brown, This Business

of Issues: Coping with the Company's Environments 15–16 (1979).

97. Allen, *Increasing Productivity in the United States: Ways in Which the Private and Public Sectors Can Contribute to Productivity Improvement,* in Productivity: The Foundation of Growth, Joint Economic Committee, 96th Cong., 2d Sess., 67, 70 (Dec. 1980).

98. Christainsen & Haveman, *The Determinants of the Decline in Measured Productivity Growth: an Evaluation,* in Productivity: The Foundation of Growth, Joint Economic Committee, 96th Cong., 2d Sess., 1, 2 (Dec. 1980).

99. Grayson, *The U.S. Economy and Productivity: Where Do We Go from Here?,* in Productivity: The Foundation of Growth, Joint Economic Committee, 96th Cong., 2d Sess., 18, 20 (Dec. 1980).

100. *U.S. Output—How It Stacks Up Against Other Nations',* U.S. News & World Report, Apr. 28, 1980, at 29.

101. Dernburg, *Stagflation: Causes and Cures,* in Stagflation: The Causes, Effects, and Solutions, Joint Economic Committee, 96th Cong., 2d Sess., 1 (Dec. 1980).

102. P. Blumberg, Inequality in an Age of Decline xi (1980).

103. R. Nisbet, History of the Idea of Progress 317–351 (1980).

104. Grayson, *The U.S. Economy and Productivity: Where Do We Go from Here?,* in Productivity: The Foundation of Growth, Joint Economic Committee, 96th Cong., 2d Sess., 18, 76, 88 (Dec. 1980); Thurow, *Where Management Fails,* Newsweek, Dec. 7, 1981, at 78; Burck, *What's in It for the Unions,* Fortune, Aug. 24, 1981, at 88; Burck, *What Happens When Workers Manage Themselves,* Fortune, July 27, 1981, at 62; Lubar, *Rediscovering the Factory,* Fortune, July 13, 1981, at 52; Burck, *Working Smarter,* Fortune, June 15, 1981, at 68; Bowen, *How to Regain Our Competitive Edge,* Fortune, Mar. 9, 1981, at 74; Rohatyn, *Reconstructing America,* The New York Review of Books, Mar. 5, 1981, at 16.

105. Thurow, *Death by a Thousand Cuts,* The New York Review of Books, Dec. 17, 1981, at 3.

106. Sheils, Leslie, & Thomas, *Reagan's Big Bull Rush,* Newsweek, March 9, 1981, at 60.

107. Fallows, *American Industry, What Ails It, How to Save It,* The Atlantic Monthly, Sept., 1980, at 35, 44.

108. Flint, *The Myth of the Lazy American,* Forbes, July 6, 1981, at 105; Morrow, *What Is the Point of Working?,* Time, May 11, 1981, at 93; Sheler, *Why So Many Workers Lie Down on the Job,* U.S. News & World Report, Apr. 6, 1981, at 71.

109. Maccoby & Terzi, *What Happened to the Work Ethic?,* in

Human Resources and Demographics: Characteristics of People and Policy, Joint Economic Committee, 96th Cong., 2d Sess., 71 (Dec. 1980).

110. Human Resources & Demographics: Characteristics of People and Policy 19 (Staff Study, Joint Economic Committee, 96th Cong., 2d Sess., Nov. 1980).

111. B. Torrey, Demographic Shifts and Projections, The Implications for Pensions i–ii (Working Paper for the President's Commission on Pension Policy, Apr. 1979).

112. Thurow, *Needed: A Spur for Savings,* Newsweek, Dec. 28, 1981, at 56; Ehrbar, *A Tax Strategy to Renew the Economy,* Fortune, Mar. 9, 1981, at 92; Carson-Parker, *The Capital Cloud over Smokestack America,* Fortune, Feb. 23, 1981, at 70; Sloan & Miles, *Showdown at Capital Gap,* Forbes, Jan. 7, 1980, at 38.

3 Pension Systems

Withdrawal of people from the work force because of age or disability occurred before World War II, and some pension systems existed before the war.[1] But social security, the principal source of pensions, dates only from the mid-1930s, and the proliferation of private pension plans occurred after the war. The Individual Retirement Account (IRA) was created by the Employee Retirement Income Security Act of 1974 (ERISA) and popularized by the Economic Recovery Tax Act[2] of 1981 (ERTA). Retirement as a significant political, economic, and social problem is a consequence of a combination of developments of the last four decades: (1) an increase in the rate of productivity and a rising standard of living; (2) the successful push by organized labor for fringe benefits, including pensions; (3) a favorable federal-tax policy on pensions, including income deduction, exemption, exclusion, and deferral devices; (4) general acquiescence in the redistribution of incomes through progressive taxes and the income-transfer (transfer-payments) system; and (5) an increase in the length of life and in the proportion of older people in the population.

A pension is in substance an *annuity*—a periodic payment of money over time. Although there are numerous sources of pensions, most of the disability and retirement pensions paid today are received by (1) people covered by social security (Old Age, Survivors, and Disability Insurance); (2) federal-, state-, and local-government civil-service employees; (3) career military personnel; (4) participants in private pension plans; (5) veterans; and (6) railroad workers.

Conventional wisdom holds that ideally retirement income should originate in three sources: social security, private pension plans, and private savings (the "three-legged stool").[3] The ideal is sometimes realized, but often a pensioner relies almost exclusively on social security for income on retirement.[4] Nearly all people with earned incomes pay social security taxes. Most people with earned incomes are employees, and their taxes are matched by taxes paid by their employers. As social security taxpayers leave the work force because of disability or advanced age, they usually qualify for social security benefits. Social security then tends to be universal in coverage. In contrast, coverage under private pension plans is far short of universal. Only half the private work force are in private pension plans, and the proportion of those in private pension plans who will in fact draw pensions is significantly lower than the proportion of those covered by social security who will in fact draw social security benefits. Qualifying for pensions under private pension plans tends to be more difficult than qualifying for benefits under social security.

Although the role of private sources of retirement income (including private savings) is not as well known as it might be, two matters are clear. First, private savings are not a primary source of retirement income for most retired people. Indeed, many retired people are dependent solely on social security benefits and various sorts of in-kind benefits,[5] such as food stamps. Second, in recent years many Americans have opted to spend rather than save. Thus, although private savings could be an important source of retirement income, Americans have shown little inclination to make private savings a source of retirement income. Whether popularization of the Individual Retirement Account will induce Americans to save voluntarily more of their incomes is not yet clear.

Social Security

The Nature of Social Security

Although social security is well known, neither the nature of social security nor the limitations of the social security system are well understood. Persons drawing social security disability or retirement benefits view their pensions as a return of social security taxes paid, just as one might view an annuity paid by a private insurance company as a return of the premiums paid for an insurance annuity contract. Social security does, of course, have an insurance element—the costs of providing benefits are borne by large numbers of social security taxpayers. But unlike insurance premiums, social security taxes are not invested in the usual sense. Although social security trust funds exist, they are not the principal source of social security benefits. At the end of 1980, total assets of the social security trust funds totaled $26.5 billion.[6] Social security benefits for 1980, including medicare, totaled $156.2 billion.[7] The social security system is a *pay-as-you-go* system—that is, taxes paid by those now working provide pensions for those who are disabled or retired. Furthermore, social security has an important *welfare* element—that is, benefits paid to those who earned lower incomes while in the work force are proportionately higher than benefits paid to those who earned higher incomes. Like other pension systems, social security provides *replacement income*—that is, income during disability or retirement that takes the place of earned income. If social security taxpayers have been barely above the poverty level throughout their working lives, social security benefits calculated without taking that circumstance into account would not keep them above the poverty level on retirement. Social security is therefore skewed to favor low-income workers. For numerous people now disabled or retired, particularly those from low-income groups, social security has proved to be a remarkably good investment because the benefits already received have surpassed many times over the social security taxes paid, including any matching taxes paid by employers.[8]

Although social security has undergone periodic changes since its beginnings in the mid-1930s, it falls far short of being a comprehensive social-insurance system. It provides disability or retirement income and health benefits under stated conditions, but it simply does not cover all the vicissitudes of life. For example, suppose that a person covered by social security dies at age forty-five after having paid social security taxes for more than twenty years. He is survived by a spouse but no children. His surviving spouse, aged forty-three, left the work force on her marriage at age twenty. She might be unskilled and without means of support. She is not entitled to social security survivors benefits based on her husband's work record because she does not meet the minimum age requirement (fifty if disabled, otherwise age sixty, with reduced benefits). Her predicament sometimes is attributed to a *gap* in social security.[9] This kind of gap is characteristic of an income-maintenance system emphasizing retirement. Suppose that a person who has paid social security taxes for thirty-five years loses his job at age fifty-five because technological changes force the closing of the plant at which he works. He is unable to find work, and he exhausts his unemployment benefits. Social security does not include job retraining. Although "fully insured for life" under social security, this unemployed person is not entitled to social security benefits at age fifty-five because he, like the widow at age forty-three, does not meet the minimum-age requirement for retirement benefits (sixty-two at the earliest, unless disabled). Briefly, social security began as a retirement-income system. It has expanded its coverage over the years to include survivors and dependents of covered workers, but it is still basically a means of providing limited replacement income when disability or old age occurs. It is not a comprehensive income-maintenance system. Rather, it is a part of the disorderly support system that has evolved in the United States since the days of Franklin D. Roosevelt's New Deal.

Social Security Benefits

With a few exceptions, being covered by social security is involuntary. Nearly everyone with earned income (as differentiated from investment income) must pay a social security tax or *contribution*, as it is euphemistically called. Only federal civilian employees, some state- and local-government employees, and some employees of nonprofit organizations are still outside the system. Unlike the federal income tax, the Federal Insurance Contributions Act (social security) permits no exemption of low incomes from taxation. The tax is a regressive tax. Both the so-called working poor and the very rich (who are unlikely to require retirement income from public sources) must pay social security taxes. Both the rate of tax and the base to which the rate applies have been increased from time to time, and both are scheduled to rise during the 1980s. If a taxpayer is an employee, his or her contribution is matched by a contribution from the employer.

Over a working life, a social security taxpayer accumulates quarters of coverage and becomes *insured* under social security. *Quarters of coverage* are calendar quarters. As might be expected, not all taxpayers who are insured have precisely the same status. For example, if a taxpayer has accumulated 40 quarters of coverage, he or she is *fully insured for life*. A taxpayer having at least 6 quarters of coverage during the 13 quarters ending with the quarter of the taxpayer's death (or the quarter of the taxpayer's entitlement to disability or retirement benefits) is *currently insured*. The social security Old Age, Survivors, and Disability Insurance program (OASDI) is administered solely by the federal government, and if an insured changes employment from time to time, status as an insured carries over from job to job. *Portability* of status is an important characteristic of OASDI, and in this respect, OASDI differs significantly from most private pension plans. Transferability of accumulated pension credits from one private pension plan to another on change of employment is exceptional.[10]

An insured is entitled to social security retirement benefits on attaining the customary retirement age of sixty-five and is entitled to reduced benefits on attaining the early-retirement age of sixty-two. An insured's spouse who is aged sixty-two or older or an insured's spouse of any age caring for a child of the insured is entitled to benefits that are half those of the insured; in addition, unmarried children of the insured under age eighteen are entitled to benefits. (An insured's unmarried child who was severely disabled before age twenty-two is entitled to benefits beyond age eighteen if the severe disability continues.) Under specified circumstances, an insured's divorced spouse is entitled to benefits, and an insured's grandchildren living with the insured are entitled to benefits. In sum, if a married insured who retires under social security has one or more children under age eighteen, social security provides benefits to the family that are intended to replace preretirement income, but there is a ceiling *(family maximum)* on total benefits paid to a family.

Under specified circumstances, a disabled insured is entitled to social security benefits irrespective of age. Social security originally paid benefits only to the insured himself on withdrawal from the work force because of age. In the late 1930s, survivors and dependents benefits were provided by amendment to the social security act, and in the mid-1950s, disability benefits were added. To qualify for disability benefits, it is necessary that the insured, among other things, demonstrate an inability to do substantial work for pay because of mental or physical disability. The disability must have lasted, or be expected to last, at least twelve months. An insured entitled to disability benefits forfeits benefits if he refuses to cooperate in efforts to rehabilitate him for reentry into the work force. Dependents of a disabled insured are entitled to dependents benefits just as dependents of a retired insured are entitled to dependents benefits.

If an insured dies before becoming entitled to benefits because of age or disability, his survivors might be entitled to benefits. Suppose that one who is fully insured dies at age thirty-five and is survived by his wife aged thirty-two and their two children not yet in their teens. Because the widow cares for children of the insured who are entitled to children's benefits, the widow is entitled to mother's benefits until the younger child attains age sixteen. Dependent parents of an insured who are age sixty-two or more are entitled to survivor benefits, and a divorced spouse is entitled to survivor benefits under specified circumstances. Survivors benefits paid to an insured's family after his death are the counterpart to dependents benefits paid to an insured's family on his retirement because of age or disability.

The primary beneficiary then of the social security Old Age, Survivors, and Disability Insurance program is the insured. Members of the insured's family who are dependent on the insured are entitled to benefits if the insured withdraws from the work force because of age or disability and receives retirement or disability benefits. If an insured dies, dependents of the insured are entitled to survivors benefits. Whether the insured is living or dead, members of the insured's family entitled to OASDI benefits based on the work record of the insured are entitled to benefits that are derivative. Because dependents and survivors benefits are derivative, both the availability of benefits and the size of benefits turn on what that work record was.

Adequacy of Benefits

At its inception, social security was not intended to provide an insured with replacement of earned income on retirement. It was intended to provide an income floor that could be supplemented from private savings to create replacement income.[11] An insurmountable difficulty with this conception of social security is that for many people in the work force, including those who work throughout their lives, it had, and continues to have, little connection with reality. Although there are undoubtedly many Americans who could save more and simply choose not to do so, some Americans never earn incomes sufficient to permit savings accumulations large enough to supplement public sources of income once they withdraw from the work force because of age. Therefore, as social security developed over time, it came to be viewed by both beneficiaries and policymakers alike as the principal source of replacement income for workers who have withdrawn from the work force because of age or disability.

Does social security provide a retired or disabled insured and his dependents with an income that approximates preretirement earned income? Are social security benefits high enough to permit a retired or disabled insured and his dependents to maintain a decent standard of living?

There has always been a ceiling on the amount of earned income to which the social security tax applies; thus social security is skewed to favor low-income workers. However, the people who have paid the maximum social security tax throughout their working lives and who receive the maximum social security retirement benefits are receiving social security benefits that do not amount to preretirement earned income. Such beneficiaries might have, however, retirement income from private pension plans or private savings that combined with social security benefits do approximate preretirement, earned income (thus fulfilling the original purpose of social security retirement benefits as an income floor). Similarly, many federal, state, and local civil-service employees not covered by social security take part-time work that qualifies them for social security benefits on retirement.[12] Because the wage base to which the social security tax applies in these cases is frequently low, social security retirement benefits are correspondingly low and do not approximate preretirement earned income. But again, because these particular social security beneficiaries also are entitled to retirement benefits from federal, state, or local civil-service pension systems (these beneficiaries are *double-dippers*), retirement income from all sources might indeed approximate preretirement earned income. Briefly, putting a ceiling on the wage base to which the social security tax applies, failing to exempt low incomes altogether from the social security tax, and skewing social security to favor low-income workers all affect the extent to which social security retirement benefits approximate preretirement, earned income. From the fact that social security retirement benefits, viewed alone, do not ap-

Pension Systems

proximate preretirement earned income, it does not necessarily follow that retirement income from all sources does not approximate preretirement earned income.

Not everyone has multiple sources of income on retirement. Millions of workers earn low or moderate incomes throughout their lives. Either they do not fall under private pension plans at all, or they do so for periods so brief that they accumulate no pension credits. Although they save sporadically, they do not accumulate savings. They do not live in poverty, and they do not regard themselves as poor, but they are nonetheless living on the edge of poverty because they do not have resources sufficient to withstand a financial crisis. For them the adequacy of social security benefits on retirement is critical since social security is their principal source, and sometimes their only substantial source, of retirement income.[13]

People retiring now at the normal retirement age of sixty-five who have earned the minimum wage during their working years are entitled to social security benefits that approach 70 percent of preretirement, earned income. Those who have earned average wages are entitled to benefits that are about 55 percent of preretirement, earned income.[14] Because living expenses are somewhat lower after retirement, it has been suggested that retired people who have earned minimum wages require about 80 percent of preretirement, earned income to maintain the preretirement standard of living.[15] Considered in this light, social security retirement benefits of low-income workers do not approximate preretirement earned income and are not replacement income.

Social security is frequently credited with keeping 14 to 15 million people (aged women, in particular) out of poverty.[16] Many social security beneficiaries who do not receive pensions from either private pension plans or public pension plans other than social security do qualify for one or more components of the income-maintenance system. The old are less healthy than the young, and for many of them, qualifying for medicare is just as important as receiving a periodic social security check. Subsidized housing and food stamps are significant sources of supplemental income.[17] In other words, although social security alone does not provide replacement income on retirement, social security as a part of the income-maintenance system is a principal source of replacement income for most people in the work force. For those who earned very high incomes and fell under private pension plans now paying generous retirement benefits and for some former civil-service employees now receiving civil-service pensions approximating preretirement, earned income, the social security retirement benefit is a bonus. But such beneficiaries are the exception, not the rule. For most beneficiaries, social security is an essential element of retirement income.

Disability Benefits

Social security disability benefits became available in the mid-1950s. Between 1965 and 1978 the number of people receiving such benefits tripled.[18] Charges were made from time to time that qualifying for disability benefits had become too easy and that some beneficiaries of disability benefits had incomes high enough to discourage their reentry into the work force even if reentry were feasible.[19] Consequently, efforts were made to tighten up the disability-insurance component of the OASDI program. The efforts have had limited success. Age is a matter of public record, but disability is not. It is therefore hardly surprising that difficulties in administering the social security disability program are less amenable to resolution than are the problems of administering the social security retirement program.

Fiscal Importance of Social Security

The structure of social security (the social security tax rate, the earned-income base to which the tax applies, and the method of calculating benefits) dictates that benefits received by an insured and an insured's dependents are limited in amount and do not approximate preretirement, earned income. Nonetheless, the fiscal importance of social security is enormous. About one of every six Americans receives social security benefits. Nearly all people sixty-five or older are covered by medicare. Because of the number of social security and medicare beneficiaries, any change in benefits is likely to have significant fiscal consequences. Annual federal expenditures for social security and medicare combined are about $180 billion,[20] and this figure has been steadily increasing. This annual outlay amounts to almost one-third of the total value of accumulated assets in public and private pension plans in the United States.

Private Pensions

Social Security and Private Pension Plans Compared

About nine of every ten people with earned incomes—about 90 million people—pay social security taxes, become insured, and qualify for social security benefits. Only half the private work force fall under private pension plans created by private employers or unions, or both private employers and unions together.[21] Of those falling under private pension plans, not all will qualify for pensions. Many private pension plans are *noncontributory*—that is, no deductions are made from employees' salaries and wages to fund the plans; rather, the sponsoring employers fund the plans. Consequently, employees might work for some years before the vesting of benefits occurs that gives a nonforfeitable right to a pension on retirement, irrespective of continuing employment. Under the Employee Retirement Income Security Act of 1974 (ERISA), which regulates nearly all private pension plans, vesting lawfully can be deferred for as much as ten years.

A record of a social security taxpayer's covered earnings is maintained by the federal government so that irrespective of changes in covered employment, quarters of coverage accumulate over time. Although portability of accumulated private pension credits from one private pension plan to another is occasionally possible on change of employment, it is still exceptional and is likely to remain so. There is great variety in private pension plans, and they do not lend themselves to portability of accumulated pension credits.

Unlike social security, which is a pay-as-you-go pension system, private pension plans are *funded* plans. Funds are accumulated on a regular basis and are usually invested by insurers (if a plan is *insured*) or by bankers (if a plan is *trusteed*). Regular funding and successful investing are intended to assure a continuing source of pension benefits. But just as social security from time to time verges on bankruptcy, so too some private pension plans encounter financial difficulties. Regular funding contributes to stability, but it does not assure it. Private pension plans, like public pension plans, depend heavily on a healthy, expanding economy.

Because social security is social insurance, benefits under the Old Age, Survivors, and Disability Insurance program were extended over time from the insured to include under specified circumstances the insured's spouse, divorced spouse, children, grandchildren, and parents. Private pension plans provide benefits for the participating employee. Whether the participant's dependents and survivors are provided for depends on the terms of the plan. Although ERISA requires that most pension plans providing retirement annuities offer a joint and survivor annuity, that is, an annuity payable to the participant for life and then to any surviving spouse, ERISA nonetheless permits the participant to reject that kind of annuity in writing, thus foreclosing benefits for the surviving spouse.[22]

Because almost all people with earned incomes must pay social security taxes, even low-income workers fall under social security. Creation of private pension plans is not required by law. Therefore, whether an employee falls under a private pension plan hinges on a number of factors. Large employers are more likely than small employers to sponsor private pension plans. Because pensions are among the fringe benefits sought by organized labor, a unionized enterprise is more likely than a nonunionized one to have a private pension plan. Although a new business might get underway with a fullfledged package of employee benefits, including private pension plan benefits, providing pensions is expensive, and pension expense might be forgone, at least initially. In sum, private pension plans are found in large, well-established, unionized businesses. The employee, particularly the low-income worker, who takes his social security quarters of coverage with him from job to job might be covered by private pension plans only sporadically, if at all.

In occasional financial difficulties or not, social security is here to stay. Private pension plans can and do fail, or *terminate,* to the disappointment of participants and their families. The impact of termination is mitigated under ERISA through the Pension Benefit Guaranty Corporation (PBGC), a nonprofit corporation administering a federal insurance program. But not all private pension plans fall under ERISA, and therefore not all are insured by PBGC.

Variety of Private Pension Plans

A *defined-benefit* pension plan specifies the pension payable on retirement or the method of calculating the pension. A *defined-contribution* plan fixes contributions to the plan, but the pension payable turns on what the accumulation in a participant's account will buy on retirement, and that turns in part on investment experience. In the United States there are about 132,000 defined-benefit private pension plans with about 34 million participants, and about 319,000 defined-contribution private pension plans with about 15.5 million participants.[23] Defined-contribution plans include employee profit-sharing plans and employee stock-ownership plans; and if American workers become so-called partners in American business to a significant extent, both the number and the importance of such benefit plans will increase. Defined-contribution plans are fully funded, are considered self-insured, and therefore do not fall under the private-pension-plan insurance program of the Pension Benefit Guaranty Corporation.

Integrating Private-Pension-Plan Benefits with Social Security Benefits

Because most employees in private pension plans also are covered by social security, some private pension plans *integrate* plan benefits with social security benefits, that is, the plans take account of the fact that a participant on retirement might draw benefits from more than one source. Simply deducting *(offsetting)* social security benefits from the benefits that otherwise would be payable under a private pension plan is the simplest way of integrating benefits. About 30 percent of all private-pension-plan participants fall under integrated plans.[24] To qualify for favorable federal-income-tax treatment under the Internal Revenue Code, a private pension plan that integrates benefits must do so in a way that does not discriminate in favor of employees who are highly paid. Although integrating benefits is consistent with treating social security retirement benefits as an income floor, integration complying with Internal Revenue Code requirements does not preclude pensions payable to high-income workers that are substantially larger than pensions payable to low-income workers. Therefore integration sometimes is viewed as unfair. But nondiscriminatory integration does not require equality of outcome. While in the work force, Americans are able to accept with relative equanimity great disparities in earned incomes ("If they can get it, why not?"). Withdrawal from the work force allows time for reflection, and many Americans find striking disparities in retirement income inappropriate and distasteful. This state of affairs is simply one more consequence of our failure (and perhaps inability) to resolve such troublesome issues as equal pay for equal work (for example, paying females the same wage as males for the same work); comparable pay for different lines of work (for example, paying public school teachers at least the same wage as plumbers); and limiting disparities in earned incomes (for example, precluding a ballplayer from earning $1 million a year while permitting an agricultural fieldworker to subsist on marginal wages). The problems of retirement income originate largely in the problems of work—wage levels, wage disparities, and job security. The disarray of the income-maintenance system can be ameliorated by systematic, continuing effort, but in the long run, improvement of the income-maintenance system will originate principally in improving the workplace.

Adequacy of Benefits

Private pensions tend to be overrated as a source of retirement income for a number of reasons. First, American workers change jobs frequently, sometimes involuntarily, but often as a matter of choice. Vesting requirements under private pension plans are onerous, and transferability (portability) of accumulated private-pension credits is exceptional. Consequently, people hired by a succession of private employers are unlikely to qualify for private pensions. Women and low-income workers fall into this group, and they subsidize pensions for those who do qualify. Second, private-pension-plan benefits replace only a fraction of preretirement, earned income—about 20 to 25 percent.[25] Third, private-pension-plan benefits are unlikely to be indexed, and they have been badly eroded by inflation. In short, private-pension-plan benefits are difficult to acquire, they are low in amount, and they do not maintain their purchasing power over time.

Economic Importance of Private Pension Plans

Not surprisingly, estimates of the total value of public- and private-pension-fund assets vary. The variation is attributable in part to difficulties of valuation in a time of financial instability. A figure of $650 billion probably is representative. About half of that figure originates in private pension plans. Managers of private-pension-plan assets—principally bankers, trust companies, and insurers—along with other institutional investors, such as trustees of college- and university-endowment funds and trustees of charitable trusts and foundations, can and do have an effect on the course of the stock market. But they are not significant sources of so-called venture capital.

Of the $15 billion paid annually to about 7 million beneficiaries of private pension plans, $12.3 billion originates in trusteed plans and $2.6 billion in insured plans.[26]

Federal-, State-, and Local-Government Pension Plans

Federal Plans

Of the nearly seventy federal retirement plans,[27] thirty-eight have been described as "major."[28] The Civil Service Retirement System (CSRS), the largest of the civilian-retirement plans, covers over 90 percent of federal civilian employees, or about 2.7 million people. Federal entities having their own pension plans include the Foreign Service, the Federal Reserve Board, and the Tennessee Valley Authority.[29]

Participants in a majority of the smaller federal retirement plans fall under social security on an additive basis, but participants in the civil-service retirement system do not. CSRS is a *contributory* pension plan, that is, it is funded through payroll deductions and (to a much greater extent) through federal-government appropriations.

Employees under CSRS are eligible for full retirement benefits at age fifty-five with thirty years of service and at age sixty with twenty years of service. Both length of service and highest earnings enter into the calculation of retirement benefits. Surviving children of participants are entitled to benefits, and participants can provide for other surviving dependents by electing to do so under options available on retirement. There is no spouse's benefit under CSRS comparable to the spouse's benefit provided under social security.

Adequacy of Federal Benefits

Federal civil-service retirement benefits are usually characterized as relatively generous, replacing 40 to 70 percent of preretirement, earned income.[30] Many civil-service employees accumulate quarters of coverage under social security by holding down second jobs or engaging in part-time self-employment. Or on retirement from federal employment, they undertake second careers that fall under social security. Consequently, they qualify for both federal civil-service pensions and social security retirement benefits and are double-dippers.

State- and Local-Government Plans

There are about 6,600 state- and local-government retirement programs covering more than 9 million employees.[31] *Local government* includes municipalities, counties, townships, and school districts. The variety of these programs rivals that of private pension plans—some are contributory and others are noncontributory, some are funded and others are unfunded. The number of employees covered ranges from less than a hundred to more than 500,000 per plan.[32] By agreement with the federal government, state- and local-government employees can be covered by social security, and about 70 percent of the 13 million state- and local-government employees fall under social security. Nearly 100 percent of state- and local-government employees have some kind of pension coverage, but just what that is depends on history. Because of constitutional inhibitions on forcing states to fall under social security, and because Congress sought to encourage voluntary social security coverage of state- and local-government employees, the matter of coverage is complicated. For example, a state employee might be covered by a state retirement plan that is *integrated* with social security. Another employee of the same state might fall under another state retirement plan that includes no social security component at all.

State and local governments that have participated in the social security program for five years can submit notice of intent to withdraw and can withdraw from the program two years after submitting notice of intent. Although withdrawals have occurred from time to time, the proportion of state- and local-government employees falling under social security has remained about the same for the last decade.

As might be expected, state-government retirement plans encompass about four-fifths of the combined membership of all state and local plans.[33] Although the number of state-government retirement plans is small as compared to the number of local-government plans, there is nonetheless great variety in state plans. For example, a state might administer a *general-coverage* plan applicable to nearly all state-government employees, and a *limited-coverage* plan applicable to employees of a particular kind—teachers, for example. At both the state and local government levels, police officers and firefighters have been singled out for special consideration under pension plans.

Eligibility for full retirement benefits under state-government plans is similar to eligibility under the federal Civil Service Retirement System, that is, it usually is based on a minimum age of sixty or sixty-five, or a minimum age plus a stipulated number of years of service. Plans covering police officers or firefighters usually provide for retirement at age fifty or fifty-five. Both length of service and highest earnings ordinarily enter into the calculation of benefits. Provision for survivors often depends on elections made by participants on retirement.

Adequacy of State and Local Benefits

Generally speaking, state- and local-government retirement benefits, like federal civil-service retirement benefits, are more generous than those paid under private pension plans.[34] Sometimes retirement income more than replaces preretirement, earned income—a state of affairs that attracts public notice and brings all pension systems into unnecessary disrepute. Like numerous federal civil-service employees, some state- and local-government employees qualify on the basis of their lifetime-employment records for pensions from more than one source.

Economic Importance of State- and Local-Government Pension Plans

Assets of state- and local-government pension plans are valued at about $200 billion, and they are increasing at the rate of 10 percent a year. Benefits are being paid to more than 2 million people.[35] Like private pension funds, state- and local-government pension funds are being scrutinized carefully as a source of financing the reindustrialization of the United States. Any significant change in the law of fiduciary administration in response to this process is likely to occur first with respect to state- and local-government pension funds.[36]

Deficiencies of Federal-, State-, and Local-Government Plans

Social security taxes originating in earned income enable a self-employed person or an employee to attain insured status under social security relatively quickly, and an insured takes this status from one covered employment to another over a working life. Just as private pension plans pose difficulties of vesting (which assures a pension irrespective of continuing employment) and portability (that is, transferability of accumulated pension credits on change of employment), so too government pension plans at all levels of government have burdensome requirements on vesting and only limited portability of pension credits. Some government pension plans are contributory, and immediate vesting does occur, but it is not unusual for state- or local-government pension plans to defer vesting for five or ten years. *Reciprocity* is an arrangement by which two or more pension plans agree to recognize years of employment under any of them. A state employee changing from one state job to another state job within the same state might find that reciprocity among state pension plans permits him to transfer his accumulated credits from one state pension plan to another, but if he were to take a state job in a different state, portability of credits would be impossible.

The problems of funding that are found in both social security and some private pension plans are also found in federal-, state-, and local-government plans. Nearly all pension systems in the United States have promised more than they can deliver based on current funding and benefit practices.[37] Those who have retired during the last twenty years or so have been fortunate in that they have retired at a time of general prosperity when pension promises could be kept because the dependency ratio is still favorable. As demands on the pension systems become heavier, the promises to some extent may go unfulfilled.

Military Pensions and Veterans Pensions

Military Pensions

Unlike most federal civil-service employees, the 2.9 million members of the armed forces have been covered by social security since the mid-

1950s and they pay social security taxes.[38] Since 1978 they have also received social security credits, limited in amount, that reflect military allowances (in-kind pay). While accumulating social security quarters of coverage, career military personnel (as differentiated from those in military service for a few years) also accumulate credits toward military pensions that are financed from general federal revenues. After thirty years of service, irrespective of age, career military personnel qualify for military pensions equaling 75 percent of final basic pay; after twenty years of service, irrespective of age, career military personnel (with the consent of the government) qualify for military pensions equaling 50 percent of final basic pay. These military pensions are supplemented by social security benefits either on retirement from military service or later (when social security eligibility requirements are met), and might be topped by private-pension-plan benefits originating in private employment after retirement from military service.

Both private employers and government employers use pension plans as a means of attracting and retaining employees, but the federal government puts special emphasis on military pensions to attract and retain career military personnel. The unique nature of military pensions received recognition by the U.S. Supreme Court in *McCarty* v. *McCarty*, 453 U.S. 210 (1981), which held that in a divorce proceeding federal law precludes a state court from dividing military retired pay pursuant to state community-property laws. The holding of *McCarty* was overturned by Congress in 1982.

Adequacy and Fiscal Importance of Military Pensions

Retired career military personnel drawing both military pensions and social security retirement benefits enjoy incomes approximating preretirement, earned incomes.[39] If supplemented by private-pension-plan retirement benefits, retirement incomes might exceed preretirement, earned incomes. Both government civil-service pensions and private pensions have *compensation* (for past service) and *reward* (for faithful service) elements. Military pensions undoubtedly have a preponderatingly heavy reward element. The reward element is defensible, but some people believe that it cannot justify retirement incomes that exceed earned incomes. The terrors of old age are frightening, but they are not the same as the terrors of the battlefield. Military retirement and survivors benefits paid to about 1.4 million people cost the federal government about $16 billion per year.[40]

Veterans Pensions and Their Fiscal Importance

People in active military service during the so-called Mexican border period or in World War I, World War II, the Korean conflict, or the Vietnam war might qualify for veterans benefits payable for service-related disabilities (the counterpart of disability benefits available under social security) or because of need unrelated to military service (the counterpart of supplemental security income). Veterans service-related benefits are considered payable as a matter of right, and veterans non-service-related benefits are considered payable as a matter of grace, but both are now firmly embedded as parts of the federal entitlement programs. Like social security, veterans benefits include survivors benefits. About 2.6 million disabled veterans receive about $8 billion per year in disability payments, and about 2.2 million other veterans and dependents receive about $3.7 billion per year in need-based payments.[41]

Railroad Pensions

Since the mid-1930s the federal government has administered a retirement plan for the railroads. In the mid-1970s, about 40 percent of railroad retirement beneficiaries also received social security benefits and received more in combined benefits—a windfall—than they would have received had they come under only one pension system. By the Railroad Retirement Act of 1974, railroad retirement benefits are coordinated with social security benefits, with protections against dual payment for the same employment. With respect to some persons, the windfall benefit was eliminated by the act. The congressional scheme for determining those who continue to qualify for the windfall benefit and those who do not withstood attack on constitutional grounds in *U.S. Railroad Retirement Board* v. *Fritz*, 449 U.S. 166 (1980). The Supreme Court held that railroad retirement benefits, like social security benefits, are not contractual and may be altered or eliminated at any time.

The railroad retirement system covers a little over half a million workers. Over a million beneficiaries—annuitants, dependents, and survivors—receive benefits of $4.2 billion per year.[42] The retirement system was established in the 1930s in response to the financial difficulties of existing railroad retirement plans. Financial problems persist. Like social security, the system faces possible bankruptcy.

Conclusion

Government Involvement in Pension Systems

Governments (federal, state, or local) directly or indirectly administer all American pension systems with the exception of private pension plans. Through the Employee Retirement Income Security Act of 1974 (ERISA), the federal government regulates private pension plans. A part or all, as the case may be, of the funds required to meet periodic payments of many pension benefits originates in the power of governments to tax. Pension systems that qualify for favorable federal-income-tax treatment through the deduction, exemption, exclusion, and deferral devices enjoy an indirect federal subsidy. Allowed tax deductions for qualified private pension plans amount to about $13 billion per year.[43]

Government sponsorship of pension systems carries two important consequences. Pensions are payable in money, and money has declined in value. When disability or retirement benefits are payable from tax revenues, a decline in the purchasing power of the pension dollar usually is offset by ad hoc increases in pension benefits or by raising benefits in accordance with a variable such as the consumer price index. Federal pensions are indexed, and some state- and local-government pensions are indexed. Although a few private pension plans have made ad hoc adjustments in benefits to offset in part the ravages of inflation, an insignificant percentage of private-pension-plan benefits are indexed. Clearly government pensioners are advantaged in this respect.[44]

Just as government sponsorship leads to a more ready response to pension deficiencies caused by inflation, so too government sponsorship leads to a more ready response to pension deficiencies of underfunding or inadequate funding. Private pension plans failed before ERISA, and private pension plans terminate under ERISA, although the consequences of termination are mitigated by the existence of the Pension Benefit Guaranty Corporation. Social security has funding problems, but a solution to those problems will be found, based principally on the power to tax (significant reduction in benefits is politically unthinkable). Again, government pensioners are advantaged in this respect.

A second consequence of government sponsorship of pension systems is the settling of pension problems by direct involvement of affected groups in the political process. No elaborate documentation is required to demonstrate the political clout exercised by elderly beneficiaries of social security when changes in social security that affect them adversely are suggested. Those seeking to use accumulated pension funds to advance particular political, social, or economic goals bring pressure on governments either to acquiesce in interpretations of law that favor their aims or to change the law to achieve their ends. In this political maneuvering, the general public interest in the maintenance of sensible pension systems is likely to be ignored.

Pensions and Chance

What a pension system is and what it offers depend on the structure of the system, and structure is largely a matter of history, including political history. Accumulating pension assets and building up pension reserves are frequently stressed as a means of assuring adequate pensions; yet career military personnel enjoy retirement incomes usually regarded as generous, and these incomes originate in the military pension system and social security, both of which are unfunded, pay-as-you-go pension systems. But military pensions are backed by the power of the federal government, including the power to tax, and retired career military personnel have powerful friends both in and out of government ready to assist in efforts to protect military pensions. Social security retirement benefits, military pensions, and veterans pensions, unlike other government pensions and private pensions, are considered sacred, and altering them significantly is politically difficult. Were the Pension Benefit Guaranty Corporation to find itself in an untenable financial position, bailout by the federal government is probable. If the Social Security Administration finds itself out of funds, federal intervention is certain.

Pension Funds as Savings

Because some pension systems include the accumulation of funds from which to pay benefits, many people falling under pension plans are required to save involuntarily—current consumption is forgone to set aside a part of earned income to be drawn on during disability or retirement. If such pension plans are contributory so that there is immediate vesting of the participants' interests, or if plans are noncontributory but vesting occurs within a few years, the savings analogy is apt. For these Americans, interests in pensions are a significant part of their net worth. It is true, of course, that during employment a participant's vested interest is beyond his control, and in that respect, it differs from more conventional kinds of savings. If employment ceases, however, a participant may, if he wishes, withdraw his interest. Social security, the most important and the most pervasive pension system, has no such savings element. Social security is social insurance. An insured under social security who is "fully insured for life" might die at age sixty-two while still employed.

Although the insured paid social security taxes every year from entry into the work force at age eighteen until the time of death, the only social security payment attributable to covered employment might be the social security death benefit of a few hundred dollars. For this insured, an interest in social security is not a significant part of net worth.

Putting Pensions into Context

Although there are some exceptions, people covered by only one pension system throughout their working lives are ill-advised to rely solely on that system for replacement of earned income on withdrawal from the work force because of disability or age. In the abstract, the retired are expected to lead a simpler life than those in the work force, and they are expected either explicitly or implicitly to accept a lower standard of living with good grace. This view of the retired has little connection with reality. The retired frequently are forced by circumstance to accept a lower standard of living, but there is no evidence that they do so voluntarily. The habits of a lifetime are difficult to change. Those who are profligate during their working years are likely to be profligate on retirement.

It follows that a pension system should be viewed in the context of the entire income-maintenance system. Although a pension alone is unlikely to provide retirement income that approximates preretirement, earned income, a pension from one system that is supplemented by a pension from another system might do so, or a pension from one system might be supplemented from one or more of the other elements in the income-maintenance system such as food stamps or subsidized housing. People often disagree on whether the availability of medicare should be considered income, but it is clear that subsidized housing is a form of income—housing is continuous whereas illness usually is sporadic. In sum, pensions are but a part of the income-maintenance system. It is convenient for particular purposes to consider them alone, but ultimately they must be viewed as simply one means by which the work force supports the dependent segments of the population.

Pensions and the Work Force

It is true that participants in some pension systems, including some systems sponsored by governments, help to fund pension benefits directly through payroll deductions earmarked for pensions, but more frequently those in the work force fund pension benefits indirectly through contributions made by their employers (forgone wages) or through tax payments that are used to build up pension funds or to pay pension benefits. Irrespective of whether the work force supports the disabled and the retired directly or indirectly, the ability of the work force to give continuing support to others depends on regular employment at a wage that both permits and encourages forgoing some consumption to allow others to share in the goods and services available for distribution from time to time. Pensions are part of the income-transfer system by which those who have incomes share with those who have lower incomes or no incomes at all. Pensions give access to goods and services, and as long as nearly all in the work force are at work, and goods and services are relatively abundant, those at work are willing to support those who are not, including the disabled and the retired. All pension systems are based on a healthy economy. No pension system remains uanffected for long by a high rate of unemployment, inflation, declining productivity, and slow economic growth. Realistically, pensioners, like other dependent segments of the population, are at the mercy of the work force.

Notes

1. B. Stein, Social Security and Pensions in Transition 68–71, 109 (1980).

2. 26 U.S.C. §§ 219, 408 (Supp. 1982), *amending* 26 U.S.C. §§ 219, 408 (1978) and related sections of the Internal Revenue Code.

3. Coming of Age: Toward a National Retirement Income Policy 12–14 (Final Report, President's Commission on Pension Policy, Feb. 26, 1981).

4. E. Meier & C. Dittmar, Income of the Retired, Levels and Sources 42, 52 (Working Paper for the President's Commission on Pension Policy, Oct. 1980).

5. *See generally* T. Borzilleri, In-Kind Benefit Programs and Retirement Income 1–23 (Working Paper for the President's Commission on Pension Policy, Oct. 1980).

6. Hildreth, *The Battle to Save Social Security*, U.S. News & World Report, July 20, 1981, at 41.

7. Pension Facts 21 (American Council of Life Insurance 1981).

8. The first social security beneficiary paid about $22 in social security taxes and drew benefits totaling about $20,000. *Your Stake in the Fight over Social Security*, Consumer Reports, Sept. 1981, at 503, 504.

9. Leonard, *The Three-Legged Stool: Women and Retirement (In) Security*, 32 Hastings L.J. 1195, 1208–1209 (1981). *See generally* Social

Security in America's Future 225–245 (Final Report of the National Commission on Social Security, Mar. 1981).

10. B. Stein, Social Security and Pensions in Transition 114 (1980). For a general discussion of the matter of portability, see E. Meier & P. Bassett, Portability of Pension Benefits 1–3 (Working Paper for the President's Commission on Pension Policy, Jan. 1981).

11. *Your Stake in the Fight over Social Security,* Consumer Reports, Sept. 1981, at 503, 505.

12. R. Tilove, Public Employee Pension Funds 108–111 (1976).

13. E. Meier & C. Dittmar, Income of the Retired, Levels and Sources 42, 52 (Working Paper for the President's Commission on Pension Policy, Oct. 1980).

14. *Your Stake in the Fight over Social Security,* Consumer Reports, Sept. 1981, at 503, 505.

15. E. Meier, C. Dittmar, & B. Torrey, Retirement Income Goals 8 (Working Paper for the President's Commission on Pension Policy, Mar. 1980).

16. *Your Stake in the Fight over Social Security,* Consumer Reports, Sept. 1981, at 503, 505.

17. *See generally* T. Borzilleri, In-Kind Benefit Programs and Retirement Income 1–23 (Working Paper for the President's Commission on Pension Policy, Oct. 1980).

18. *The Beneficent Monster,* Time, June 12, 1978, at 24, 26–27.

19. The General Accounting Office estimated that in January 1981 about half a million people not currently disabled were receiving about $2 billion in disability payments. *From the Schools to the Sewers,* Time, Mar. 2, 1981, at 16, 18.

20. *From the Schools to the Sewers,* Time, Mar. 2, 1981, at 16, 18; *Spending for the Elderly: The Dollars Pile Up,* U.S. News & World Report, July 20, 1981, at 43; *Backing Down on Benefits,* Time, Oct. 12, 1981, at 32, 42.

21. Social Security and Pensions: Programs of Equity and Security 16 (Staff Study, Joint Economic Committee, 96th Cong., 2d Sess., Oct. 1980).

22. 26 U.S.C. § 401 (1978); 29 U.S.C. § 1055 (1975).

23. Pension Facts 5 (American Council of Life Insurance 1981).

24. Social Security and Pensions: Programs of Equity and Security 18 (Staff Study, Joint Economic Committee, 96th Cong., 2d Sess., Oct. 1980).

25. *Id.* 22–23.

26. *Id.* 16–17.

27. S. Ross, Income Security Programs: Past, Present and Future 26 (Working Paper for the President's Commission on Pension Policy, Oct. 1980).

28. Social Security and Pensions: Programs of Equity and Security 12 (Staff Study, Joint Economic Committee, 96th Cong., 2d Sess., Oct. 1980).

29. For an overview of the ten largest federal pension plans, see Federal Pension Programs 1–11 (Working Paper for the President's Commission on Pension Policy, Jan. 1981).

30. Social Security and Pensions: Programs of Equity and Security 12 (Staff Study, Joint Economic Committee, 96th Cong., 2d Sess., Oct. 1980).

31. Funding of State and Local Government Pension Plans: A National Problem 2 (Report to the Congress by the Comptroller General of the United States, Aug. 30, 1979); B. Jump, Jr., The Future of State and Local Pensions 1 (Final Report for Depts. of HUD, HHS, and Labor, National Institute of Education, and President's Commission on Pension Policy, Apr. 1981).

32. Employee Pension Systems in State and Local Government 3 (Tax Foundation, Inc., 1976).

33. *Id.* 4.

34. B. Jump, Jr., The Future of State and Local Pensions 1–26 (Final Report for Depts. of HUD, HHS, and Labor, National Institute of Education, and President's Commission on Pension Policy, Apr. 1981).

35. *Id.* 1.

36. See Final Report, Governor's Public Investment Task Force 5–7 (State of California, Oct. 1981).

37. Social Security and Pensions: Programs of Equity and Security 28–30 (Staff Study, Joint Economic Committee, 96th Cong., 2d Sess., Oct. 1980).

38. *Id.* 14.

39. *Id.*

40. *Putting the Budget in Perspective,* U.S. News & World Report, Feb. 15, 1982, at 18, 19; *Tax and Budget Cuts: What to Expect from Congress,* U.S. News & World Report, Feb. 2, 1981, at 57, 58.

41. *After 50 Years, VA's Job Is Just Beginning,* U.S. News & World Report, June 16, 1980, at 81.

42. Social Security and Pensions: Programs of Equity and Security 14 (Staff Study, Joint Economic Committee, 96th Cong., 2d Sess., Oct. 1980).

43. *Id.* 18.

44. Quinn, *Bloated Military Pensions,* Newsweek, June 21, 1982, at 56; Hildreth & Morse, *"The Great COLA War"—What's at Stake,* U.S. News & World Report, Apr. 26, 1982, at 90.

4 Pensions in the Changing Wealth-Transmission Process

The conventional law on the devolution of private wealth—the law of property, trusts, wills, future interests, and administration of estates—presupposes acquisition of property (through work, gift, inheritance, theft, or chance) and its accumulation, conservation, taxation, and transmission from generation to generation, almost exclusively within the family. Traditionally, such gifts are made during the lifetime of a donor and at his death to the spouse, children, parents, other relatives, and (to a limited extent) charity.

Some groups within the population who are politically and economically important have minimal interest in the private wealth-transmission process because they have little wealth and cannot accumulate it in significant quantities. The law permits any person of sufficient age having "testamentary capacity" to execute a will, irrespective of whether he has property or a reasonable expectation of acquiring property. But it is the decedent leaving a *net probate estate* who engages our attention. Even if it is difficult to separate the so-called working class from the middle class,[1] it is the middle class and the rich who have a principal interest in the law of property, trusts, wills, future interests, administration of estates, and death taxes.

If it is true that the poor will always be with us, it might also be true that that rich will always be with us. If so, we can be reasonably confident that some part of the population, however small, will continue to use traditional property devices (for example, trusts with class gifts and powers of appointment) to direct the devolution of wealth from generation to generation. But what of that much more numerous group—the middle class? What is happening to them and their families in the last decades of the twentieth century that affects their desire and ability to acquire, accumulate, and conserve wealth that might be transmitted during life or at death? What is happening to the legal doctrines and the legal devices that they have traditionally used to transfer wealth? How are they affected by the proliferation of pensions and by taxation, inflation, and demographic change?

This chapter was published as R.J. Lynn, *Estate Planning: Goodbye to Wills, Trusts, and Future Interests,* in 39 Ohio St. L.J. 717 (1978). Copyright © 1978 by The Ohio State University. Reprinted by permission.

The Family

The Self-Sufficient Spouse

One observable change in the family is that the surviving spouse may be self-supporting at the death of his or her mate.[2] Since World War II women have entered the work force in ever-increasing numbers, and many women in the work force are married. The conventional view of the widow of middle age cast adrift without skills on the death of her husband still applies, of course, to numerous cases, but it is becoming less accurate than it was in the first half of this century. When both husband and wife are employed over an appreciable period of time, it is possible that both might feel obligated to acquire and accumulate wealth in order to leave to the survivor of the marriage property sufficient for comfortable support without the necessity of continuing employment. But it is also possible that if employment during the customary working years becomes the norm for both partners to a marriage, the obligation to provide for the survivor will be less keenly felt. If perceptions of diminished obligation to the spouse exist generally or if they exist with respect to particular kinds of marriages such as the companionate marriages of the elderly, such perceptions will ultimately be reflected by revision of *forced-share* statutes in common-law states.[3]

The Absent Spouse

When only one of the marriage partners is employed, the nature of his or her employment may require temporary absences from the home that put a strain on the marriage. That strain is increased when better career opportunities permit and at times require (under employer pressure) a change of domicile that is a wrench to both spouse and children.[4] If both husband and wife are employed, the frequency of employment-related family disruptions increases. Circumstances may require maintaining two households, one where the husband works and one where the wife works. Such physical separation might make the heart grow fonder, with a corresponding desire to afford comfortable support for a surviving spouse. On the other hand, it might simply reinforce a disinclination to accumulate wealth to leave to one who has been self-sufficient throughout the marriage.

Successive Marriages

Successive marriages, whether originating in divorce or originating in death, have always complicated property arrangements of some families.

But so-called no-fault divorce statutes are now common, and within all age groups in the married population, divorce has increased in frequency. About one out of two marriages ends in divorce.[5] Marriage tends to be viewed as tentative. If it does not work out, the tendency is to escape an unsatisfactory union and try again. The stigma associated with divorce has almost disappeared, and in some connections, such as employment, divorce is irrelevant. To the extent that marriage is viewed as experimental, it is likely that the motive to provide for a surviving spouse is diminished.

The matter of successive marriages originating in divorce aside, there are successive marriages that occur in a different context. The average life span in the United States has been increasing. If the marriage of an aging couple survives incompatibility, it will nevertheless be ended at some time by death. The survivor of the couple may live on for years—literally alone unless a new marriage can be entered into. Although an aging widow or widower might indeed find companionship with children and grandchildren, moving in with the next younger generation is not viewed as the solution to the economic, social, and emotional needs of older Americans. The elderly often find companionship with their own kind or they do not find it at all. Companionship frequently leads to marriage.

In these companionate marriages, motive to provide for the survivor is not merely weak; it is frequently and candidly altogether absent. Each of the partners to the marriage may be economically self-sufficient. Each may have a family or families originating in prior marriages. Though affection for the newly acquired spouse may indeed be deep, it is often insufficient to make him or her a favored object of substantial lifetime or after-death gifts. Such gifts are reserved for relatives by blood. Under these circumstances, execution of the antenuptial property agreement often equals in importance the performance of the marriage ceremony itself.

Termination of the Parent-Child Relationship

Successive marriages among the young, regardless of cause, frequently result in "his" or "her" children, "my" children, and "our" children. Because the infant mortality rate in the United States is relatively low, children of successive marriages are likely to survive dissolution of the marriages that produce them. But a child's survival of the dissolution of the marriage that produced him does not assure him a continuing connection with his parents. The child may be in effect rejected by both parents. If not rejected by both, he may in the long run be rejected by one, and in that event, may or may not formally enter the family of a stepparent through adoption. In short, successive marriages may effectively cut off a parent from one or more of his children. To the extent that a child becomes a stranger to his natural parent, the desire of the parent to provide for the child diminishes. Eventually, the desire ceases altogether, though it might be revived by the preference for the bloodline that permeates all gratuitous transfers and appears to be particularly strong at death.

Erosion of the Parent-Child Relationship

Children's Rights. This is a time of rights—the rights of those accused of crime, of prisoners, of victims, of minorities, of women, of the mentally disabled, of the physically handicapped, of the aged, of the terminally ill, and of children.[6] The unborn have not fared well in this connection since the development of their rights has been subordinated to a new-found constitutional right to privacy.[7]

Parents who would try to assure a formal education to their children seldom think twice about the state's insistence on learning to read and write. But parents who would give to their children as much privacy as possible within the home might still try to prevent a minor daughter from procuring an abortion without their consent.[8] Children's rights often are established at the expense of parents and teachers. Parents deprived by law of control over their children to an extent that parents believe to be unjustified might, logically, demand that the deprivation of authority be accompanied by a reduction in obligation.

If the development of children's rights results in both frequent assertion of such rights and a corresponding diminution in the felt obligation of parents to support their children, then irrespective of the rationality of parents' attitudes toward children's rights, there is likely to be a diminution in the felt obligation to provide for support of children through the more traditional legal devices (life insurance, trusts, and wills) after a parent's death. Any felt obligation is of course irrelevant with respect to newer wealth-transmission devices such as social security, where the covered taxpayer's choice of beneficiaries has been made for him by Congress.

Custodial Care of Children. Parents from rich families and parents from working-poor families in the United States frequently share a common characteristic—they do not raise their children. Rich parents delegate this task to surrogate parents, often conveniently removed from the immediate geographical area. Similarly, for generations the mother forced by poverty to enter the work force has entrusted the care of her small children to relatives and friends, to older children within the family, and to the streets.

Parents separated from their children by choice or by necessity can and do retain affection for them, and vice versa, but the threats to family integrity posed by separation require no elaborate documentation. Children of the rich whose parents shunt them aside may reciprocate with bitterness, and children of the poor separated by necessity from their parents may feel cheated, and they are.

This unsatisfactory pattern of child raising among some families might become the norm. Many married women work out of necessity and many others work by choice.[9] Many working women, married, divorced, or never married, are mothers of infants or young children. What happens during the working day (or night) to these children from *nuclear* families, consisting simply of parents and children, as opposed to *extended* families, including grandparents, uncles, and aunts? Some, of course, are in school. Others are turned over to custodians (sitters in the home, daycare centers outside the home).[10] There is, of course, great variation in the quality of custodial care given to children, just as there is great variation in the quality of custodial care given to other dependent segments of the population. However, it is at least doubtful that the best custodial care of infants and children matches in quality the care given to them by attentive parents.

Transmission of private wealth from generation to generation occurs almost exclusively within families. The gift to charity is still the exception, not the rule. Affection of a parent for his child motivates accumulation of wealth for the benefit of the child, and affection of a child for his parent motivates a child to contribute to the support of his parent if that need arises. To the extent that custodial arrangements for the care of infants and children diminish affection between parents and children, motive in either generation to provide for the other is adversely affected.

Rise of Family Specialists. When factory production displaced handicraft production, nonagricultural families ceased to be together during the day. The father, in particular, is absent from the home, sometimes for several days at a time, and the brunt of what is now called parenting falls on the mother unless she too has joined the work force. The task of raising children, whether by both parents or one, has been alleviated by the rise of family specialists.

Metropolitan areas abound in psychiatrists, psychologists, social workers, and family counselors, all of whom attempt to assist in the resolution of problems that once were solved principally by parents, if solved at all. Sometimes these family specialists are employed on a regular or consulting basis by schools and family-aid agencies.

To the extent that family specialists are successful in resolving difficulties that disrupt families, it is arguable that they build family solidarity and indirectly encourage intrafamily wealth transfers. But it at least can be hypothesized that family specialists have contributed to the disintegration of the family by unnecessarily taking on functions that were once performed by parents.[11]

Prevalence and Removal of Grandparents

If divorce of a child's parents does not cut the child off from a set of his natural grandparents, he is likely to have a complete array, particularly if he is among the older children in his family. Advancements in the control of the more insidious diseases, a general rise in the standard of living, and the slow but steady elimination of so-called killing jobs assure to most Americans now alive a comparatively long life span, certainly of a length sufficient to qualify many for the role of grandparent.

Will such grandparents be geographically close to their children and grandchildren? Will such grandparents be supported wholly or in part by their children?

As indicated previously in connection with the changing role of the wife, mobility is a characteristic of American family life. During infancy, children may move frequently with their parents as employment opportunities arise or dictate, and such moves frequently deprive grandparents of regular contact with their grandchildren.

As children approach maturity, the lives of their parents may achieve geographical stability as the testing period for an employed parent draws to a close. But this stability of the parents might be more than offset by a desire of retired grandparents to live in the Sunbelt states. At a time when the extended family could realistically be together (if that is an objective), separation might continue.

Suppose grandparents prefer proximity to children and grandchildren? Can they expect to achieve it by occupying a dwelling with them and taking meals in common? An idealized view of a venerated grandparent with a special place in the family is familiar. We simply do not know the extent to which that idealization mirrored reality in the past. But there is evidence that the grandparents of today and hereafter should not assume that the idealization is likely to be attained too often. The grandparents' desire for a home in common might be shared by their young grandchildren, but the desire for such proximity is not a part of the fulfillment of the middle generation that would be affected by such a living arrangement.

In sum, unless living patterns change, grandparents and grandchildren are likely to lead lives of separation. To the extent that wealth transfers turn on establishing and maintaining close family ties, factors militating against the creation of extended families diminish the frequency and quantity of intrafamily gifts.

The Contemporary Wealth-Transmission Process

Taught Law and Legal Doctrine

What is happening to the law of property, trusts, wills, future interests, and administration of estates? What are the implications of the trends?

The courses of instruction offered in law schools originate in attempts at logical differentiation, adherence to tradition, and agreement among those perceived to be principally affected by curriculum (including teachers). For years law schools offered distinct courses in trusts, wills, future interests, and administration of estates. There was, inevitably, some overlap in these courses. For example, future interests (including powers of appointment) are important features of the family trust. Administration of estates at times requires inquiry into the kinds of interests created by the testator, with important decisions on whether to give a beneficiary possession, and if so, under what conditions.

In part in response to a desire for efficiency, and in part in response to the necessity for accommodating new, important courses in the curriculum (for example, labor law and taxation), traditional property courses have been both compressed into fewer classroom hours (with correspondingly less course credit) and combined into fewer offerings. There is nothing extraordinary in this. After all, there were once law school courses in *bailments* (delivery of goods in trust) and *carriers* (transporters), and in the more superb law school library collections, there are treatises on *dilapidations* (letting buildings go to ruin) and *forestalling* (preventing normal trading) both being of sufficient interest at some time to have encouraged publication. Property law that is not taught in schools or that is not encountered in life with sufficient frequency to give it vitality, whether taught or not, finally ceases to be law at all.

As less of traditional property law is taught, new property notions become part of taught law: workers-compensation rights, unemployment-compensation rights, social security rights, pension rights, welfare rights, and so on. New forms of property do not necessarily have the attributes of the more traditional forms. For example, new forms may be less transferable either voluntarily or involuntarily. Nonetheless, and as one might expect, new forms of property carry both the benefit and the burden of conventional terminology. For example, a purpose of the Pension Reform Act of 1974 (Employee Retirement Income Security Act, or ERISA) was to assure "early vesting" of private-pension rights.[12] The exegesis of early vesting appeared with the development of the *destructibility rule*—a rule of property law that exists in just a few American jurisdictions today. Even so, one with a vested right in property certainly has at least an emotional edge on a competing claimant whose right is merely "contingent."

State law has sporadically accommodated itself to development of new property devices and to shifts in forms of property. For example, statute facilitates the use of will substitutes such as "Totten" trusts. Statute routinely exempts pension trusts from restrictive rules of property. As the tax bite looms ever larger, states adopt statutes intended to assure their residents any benefits made available to federal taxpayers from the periodic tinkerings with the Internal Revenue Code. And improvement of traditional property law is a continuing process: witness the drafting and adoption of the Uniform Probate Code.

The law of property then is still very much alive. The familiar words *vested, contingent,* and *alienable* are still very much in use. But some property doctrines are simply dying out. Although *ancestral property* is still sensibly mentioned to law students,[13] it is of no interest to the lawyer representing the retired employee whose pension benefit has been destroyed through pension-fund mismanagement and who must now look to the Pension Benefit Guaranty Corporation for relief, if indeed he is fortunate enough to fall under its shelter. Property law is with us, but it is not the property law of nineteenth-century America, and the context of property doctrine has shifted remarkably in just one generation.

The Wealth-Transmission Process

With respect to those who do transmit property to dependents and successors, what are the devices used to carry out transmission?

Many still use traditional devices, that is, the will and the trust. But to an increasing extent, wealth now is transmitted by contractual devices or by traditional property devices that have been adapted to the contemporary emphasis on avoiding probate, transmission by groups, and property management by professionals.

Life Insurance. Insuring one's life as a means of providing for dependents and successors is not a new idea. But the prevalence of group life insurance as an incident to employment assures an estate to many who would otherwise leave nothing at death. The proceeds of such insurance seldom pass through the estate of the life insured to be administered by the probate court, although proceeds might indeed be part of the estate of the life insured for death tax purposes.

Bank Arrangements. Banks have created a number of highly popular account arrangements based on the joint tenancy at common law, the third-party beneficiary contract, and the trust: the *joint* account with the incident of survivorship, the *pay-on-death* bank account, and the Totten trust. Banks service the sale of U.S. savings bonds registered in forms that include *coownership* and pay-on-death forms. Again, these devices are intended to avoid probate, and they often do, but they may be subject to claims of a surviving spouse under forced-share statutes, and they carry no federal-estate-tax advantage. *Custodial* accounts that are a feature of gifts-to-minors acts facilitate both lifetime and testamentary transfers to minors.[14]

Pensions. Pension plans (other than social security), whether funded or unfunded, whether government or private, cover many employees. Some funded plans are *insured* (so that the investment of accumulated funds is carried out by insurers) and some are *trusteed* (so that investment is carried out principally, though not exclusively, by bankers). Benefits payable under pension plans go to the covered employee himself (the participant) upon his disability or retirement, and frequently to his dependents. Benefits payable under pension plans are seldom a part of the participant's probate estate, and under some circumstances they escape death taxes.

Wealth transmitted under pension plans differs from wealth transmitted in more conventional ways in that benefits are encouragingly channeled to members of the immediate family. For example, under the Pension Reform Act of 1974, a married participant in a pension plan falling under the act is presumed on retirement to select a joint and survivor retirement benefit (covering both the participant and his spouse) unless he intentionally chooses otherwise.[15]

To put the self-employed and employees not covered by pension plans on a rough parity with participants in tax-qualified pension plans, Congress created *Keogh* plans and Individual Retirement Accounts (IRAs). By the Economic Recovery Tax Act of 1981 (ERTA), IRAs were made available to those already covered by other pension plans.

Medical Benefits. Health-care plans evolved along with pension plans.

The variety of health-care plans mirrors the variety of pension plans.[16] The growth of these plans for the benefit of the working population, whether sponsored by business employers, by unions, or by governments-as-employers, was paralleled by the creation of medicare and medicaid for the dependent nonworking population.

Although experience with health-care plans has been far from satisfactory, the tendencies are to expand the categories of disorders covered and to extend benefits to additional categories of beneficiaries. These tendencies may find further expression if National Health Insurance is adopted.

Participation in pension plans blunts the desire to accumulate wealth for disposition during retirement years. Similarly, participation (or expectation of participation) in health-care plans blunts the inclination to set aside funds to meet medical expenses during both working years and retirement years.

Charity. It is occasionally remarked that charity is "big business" in the United States. Americans are generous in sharing their wealth with the less fortunate, both at home and all over the world.[17] This continuing generosity tends to obscure what has occurred during the last half-century with respect to aiding the poor and the afflicted, improving health, and supporting education and religion through charity.

First, and of fundamental importance, is the shift from quasi-public institutional arrangements (charitable trusts and foundations, religious and educational groups) to governmental arrangements for identifying nonreligious charitable needs and affording support through expenditure of general revenues raised principally by the federal income tax. Annual expenditures by the Department of Health and Human Services account for an ever-increasing share of the federal budget.

Second, as government established its dominance in dispensing welfare, charitable trusts and foundations have tended to abandon traditional charitable activities and to shift to encouraging studies of contemporary life and to supporting nongovernmental alternatives to governmental intervention into everyday life.[18] Charitable trusts and foundations have become important, influential elements of the "third sector" that complements the public and private sectors of society.[19]

Ownership in Common. Ownership in common of some kinds of property is taken for granted by Americans. The public square with its array of buildings, sculptures, and plazas is just as familiar as the privately owned, single-family, detached dwelling. Free access to highways, roads, parks, lakes, and rivers is seldom debated, and sometimes simply not realistically debatable. Art galleries, sports arenas, and battlefields are all owned by the public, or by quasi-public charitable trusts and foundations. We treasure private property, but we have always, in some way, supported some ownership in common.

Despite sporadic efforts by government (particularly the federal government) to divest itself of land holdings, ownership in common is likely to increase, not decrease. The knowledge that both our natural and our man-made environment is a part of our heritage is no longer confined to a few eccentrics. There are reasonable differences over what constitutes our common heritage and how we should assure it to our successors, but a genuine public concern for wildlife conservation, historic preservation,[20] restoration of residential neighborhoods,[21] acquisition of scenic easements and the like, is unmistakable. Old buildings are being rescued from imminent demolition and recycled for contemporary use.[22] Natural areas suitable for recreation are being identified and acquired or set aside for public use.[23] We are learning that quality of life is desirable not only for our physical health but also for our peace of mind.

As we identify and conserve elements of our common heritage, distinctions between private and public ownership become less distinct. It is neither politically desirable[24] nor economically feasible to extend outright government acquisition much further than it is today. Therefore, to achieve ownership in common of parts of our common heritage, some aspects of private ownership are being attenuated, and the attenuation becomes public property. For example, the owner of a structure in a residential area might find himself with the right to maintain and to modify but without the right to destroy.

To the extent that we are able to extend ownership in common in a sensible and generally acceptable way, we affect the desire to acquire and transmit property privately. A nature preserve accessible to many serves much the same purpose as the privately owned rural retreat or second home, and at less cost per person to those who enjoy it. Public ownership of property will not displace private ownership, but both notions are undergoing refinement, and the refinement will affect the law of property, wills, trusts, future interests, and administration of estates.

Persistence of the Familiar. Shifting to new forms of property does not eliminate familiar problems. Thirty years ago the divorcing wife in a common-law state might sensibly seek the family home when working out an appropriate property settlement. The divorcing wife of the 1980s will also seek a share of her husband's pension rights. (In community-property states, pension rights accruing during marriage are community property.)[25] And the shift to new property devices and new forms of property does not eliminate either the need for or the persistence of experts and functionaries. On the contrary, they have multiplied many times. Lawyers, accountants, insurers, actuaries, bankers, and investment advisors are complemented by an army of bureaucrats engaged in assembling information, assessing claims, investigating abuses, and distributing benefits.[26] From top to bottom, all these people have a stake in complexity and confusion—their livelihoods depend on it.

The Context of Wealth Transmission

Taxes, Income Transfers, and Inflation

Although income levels in the United States have risen since World War II, rising incomes have been accompanied by higher expectations of what constitutes happiness, by greater demands for government services (and thus higher taxes), and by inflation.

People already retired who depend on fixed-dollar pension benefits find them less and less adequate as prices for food and shelter rise. An employer touting a proposed retirement plan may encounter prospective participants who are skeptical of pension promises because of the unsatisfactory pension experience of a parent, other relative, or acquaintance. Even a skilled acquirer and dedicated accumulator of wealth may find that his inclination to conserve wealth for his own retirement and for transmission to dependents and successors is affected by his inability to invest to keep abreast of inflation.

To the extent that one spends more on consumer goods to achieve happiness, he saves less. If a personal expenditure for services is shifted to an expenditure by government to provide services, the expenditure is financed either immediately or ultimately by taxes, including taxes on those who would prefer to forgo the expenditure. Although it is the federal income tax that exasperates taxpayers and provides unlimited source material for standup comedians, mounting federal expenditures and rising federal taxes have been paralleled by increased expenditures and higher taxes at the state and local levels.[27] Tax dollars pay for such conventional services as police protection and also support the intricate income-transfer (or transfer-payments) system[28] that includes such elements as social security[29] (both the traditional retirement and disability systems and the more recent supplementary-income system), aid to families with dependent children, and food stamps.[30]

If a person having income sufficient to give a choice of saving or spending perceives himself (correctly or incorrectly) as overburdened by taxes, unfairly saddled with an income-transfer system, beset by inflation,[31] and having less real income than he had a decade ago, he might choose to spend rather than save, especially if accumulated wealth would pass to those who, he feels, might not appreciate it anyway.

Demographic Changes

Americans now retired or approaching retirement are fortunate in this respect: A high proportion of the total population is of working age and is in the work force, and in particular, the numerous children of the baby boom following World War II are now helping to support the elderly while supporting themselves and their own families. But the population profile has been changing and is still changing.[32] Although our total population continues to grow, people are tending to live longer, and the fertility rate of American women has fallen. For some time to come, there will be a larger proportion of the old in the population and a smaller proportion of the young. The numerous children of the baby boom who now help to support the elderly will themselves age and approach retirement, followed by a generation relatively less numerous and therefore relatively more burdened in supporting the old, the disabled, the young, the unemployed, and the poor.

How will demographic changes and contemporary American living patterns affect the course of pension payments? Evidence continues to accumulate that many pension plans are in a precarious state, and expectations of some present and prospective retired people are unrealistic. The elderly may have less income than they had in their preretirement years, but they still have the vote and ample time for organizing to use it effectively. If pension benefits are threatened and the elderly take political action, what is the likely response?

As long as prosperity continues and the dependency ratio is favorable, the work force is likely to acquiesce in providing goods and services to the elderly in quantities sufficient to afford them something beyond mere subsistence. But the acquiescence might become grudging. This is a time of rising expectations. Provision by the work force for the dependent elderly and the dependent young requires those working to forgo consumption themselves. Although an occasional "return to the soil" or a simple, spare, uncomplicated existence receives attention from the media, there is no evidence that either is representative of contemporary American life. On the contrary, the emphasis is on living now and living well. To the extent that those in the work force perceive their own minimum needs as encompassing what their predecessors of a generation ago would have considered unnecessary and debilitating luxuries, provision for dependents old and young is likely to be affected adversely. If contemporary attitudes toward achieving the good life persist, and the dependency ratio becomes less favorable, this adverse effect will simply become more pronounced.

Improving the Wealth-Transmission Process

How can we improve the contemporary wealth-transmission process? First, we can try to assure that existing pension and health-care plans, whether public[33] or private,[34] whether government or nongovernment, whether fully funded or unfunded, fulfill the purpose that is the only justification for their existence—providing benefits to the retired, the disabled, and to dependents of participants in plans.

Although supervision by government of pension-plan operation is frequently suggested as a means of assuring pension benefits, it is clear that reliance on government alone may not be entirely adequate. Government might indeed be an enforcer, but government can be a source of loss to pension funds. Any state legislator or member of Congress seeking funds to finance his favorite scheme for the improvement of the human condition can point to pension funds as a source of financing, no matter how precarious the security offered the beleaguered lender.

Where the role of government as enforcer has been clearly established by law, the record of government as a supervisor of pension-plan operation is poor. The influence of organized crime over investments of Teamsters' Pension Funds is notorious. Yet years after the passage of the Pension Reform Act of 1974, it is clear that criminal influence has not been removed from the Teamsters' Pension Fund operations.[35]

The Pension Benefit Guaranty Corporation was created by the Pension Reform Act of 1974 to underwrite payment of benefits to beneficiaries of covered private pension plans that fail.[36] Although one cannot fault using the insurance device to mitigate the harshness of loss of promised benefits, the Pension Benefit Guaranty Corporation is a palliative for a disease that is largely preventable. Some promises of future benefits are unrealistic when made: The promisor has neither the resources to pay pensions over an appreciable period of time to those covered employees at or approaching retirement age when the plan is adopted nor the prospect of revenues sufficient to support pension payments to those employees retiring in years to come. It bears emphasis here that the sweep of the Pension Reform Act of 1974 does not extend to all existing pension plans, and pension plans can be adopted that do not fall within the ambit of the act.

If government is unreliable as an exclusive source of protection for pension funds, and the Pension Benefit Guaranty Corporation is an after-the-loss palliative administered at the expense of participants in successful pension plans and stockholders, to whom or to what does the participant turn for the assurance that the benefit promised him will in fact be paid?

Policing Pensions

The truth is that there is no one to turn to for such assurance. Viewed realistically, a claim to a pension or to health-care benefits is a claim to such goods and services as are available for distribution from time to time. If there are no goods and services for distribution, the claim is worthless. If beneficiaries are denied equality of access to such goods and services as are available for distribution, the value of the benefit is diminished.

Although a person approaching retirement who has vested rights in a funded pension plan has a case for equality of access to goods and services that is legally and emotionally more attractive than that of his counterpart under an unfunded pension plan, both are in fact at the mercy of the work force. In this respect, their situation is like that of minors and incompetents. They are heavily dependent on goodwill and prevailing notions of fairness. Effectiveness of the pension and health-care devices turns in the long run on a consensus that the younger, productive segments of the population will support not only themselves but also the retired and the disabled. Yet many in the work force, preoccupied with trying to maintain themselves and improve their own position, are not particularly interested in the difficulties of pensioners even though they themselves are not far removed from retirement age.[37] Because people enter the work force every year, some who produce the goods and services available for distribution were unborn when an existing, functioning pension and health-care plan was adopted. They may be ignorant of its original justification, and resentful of the benefits it affords. In sum, a consensus existing in times of comparative prosperity may dissolve under the pressures of self-interest in times of adversity.

In the long run, the sources of assurance that pension and health-care benefits will be paid are (1) awareness of what they are; (2) general continuing acceptance of the notion that the work force will adequately support those who because of age or other disability cannot work; and (3) continuing scrutiny by participants of all devices (government or nongovernment) intended to provide pensions and like benefits. Both understanding what benefits are and effective continuing scrutiny of plans, require informed participants. Here, newspapers, periodicals, books, and television play a part. And the quality of information afforded the participants and the general public and the continuity of flow of quality information can be improved by a sustained interest in such matters by the third sector—that is, the charitable trusts and foundations sponsoring detached, scholarly inquiries into contemporary problems and institutions.

Avoiding Probate

Devices to avoid probate are not new. They are rediscovered from time to time, and the list of devices is occasionally modified. Because avoiding probate is an important objective to so many people, the legal problems associated with the process have been considered for years. Resolution of problems has been piecemeal. When public policy is clear, resolution tends to be clear-cut. For example, devices intended to avoid probate carry no federal-estate-tax advantage. In contrast, the surviving spouse electing to take a share of the estate against the will might not be able to augment the estate for such purposes by including nonprobate assets because a jurisdiction simply prohibits such inclusion. There is lack of uniformity in this connection because public policy on protecting the surviving spouse has not been settled. Similarly, the position of creditors with respect to a tenancy by the entirety varies considerably, depending on the jurisdiction.

Clarification of the characteristics of devices to avoid probate is likely to proceed slowly. General public interest in clarification does not exist. Interest of specialists is inevitably sporadic. Rarely can a specialist spend full time on improving the law.

Furthermore, the effort required to achieve consensus on the characteristics of devices is frequently deemed disproportionate to the benefits achieved. Therefore, it is probable that the most that can be accomplished is discussion and settling of policy on an item-by-item basis. For example, if it is agreed that a revocable trust is like a will for death tax purposes, it might be agreed that is it like a will for purposes of creditors' claims.

Charity

Charity needs protection from government,[38] and protection by government. In other words, charity needs protection from the ability of government to inhibit or destroy charity, and at the same time charity needs protection by government from fraud and abuse.

Because of misuse of the charitable-foundation device in the 1950s and 1960s, Congress by the Tax Reform Act of 1969[39] enacted legislation that is largely defensible and beneficial but that in part is unnecessarily punitive. Charity is a useful alternative to government action, and it has the sanction of a long tradition in areas where government has been at times hostile, ineffective, or indifferent. The punitive aspects of the Tax Reform Act of 1969 should not be used as prototypes for further legislation that in effect inhibits or destroys charity.[40] To a considerable extent, charity exists by grace of the tax laws, and tax laws are subject to change.

Because the identity of charitable objects shifts from time to time, and because charity depends heavily on regular contributions from donors, both fund raising by charities and expenditure of funds by charities have been the source of abuse. It is in this connection that charities need protection by government, for government has or can create machinery for policing both fund raising and charitable expenditures.[41] Self-policing by charities assists but cannot displace policing by government because the more flagrant charity frauds are perpetrated by those who do not participate in self-policing.

However, just as government is unreliable as an exclusive protector of pension funds, so too government is unreliable as an exclusive protector of charity. As with pension funds, protection of charity depends in the long run on informed, interested, active contributors who pay attention to the disposition of their charitable contributions.

Conclusion

Although the law of property, including the law of trusts, wills, future interests, and administration of estates, has a stability that is not shared by all other areas of law, it cannot be assumed that transmission of wealth from generation to generation in the last quarter of the twentieth century takes substantially the same form that it took in the first quarter of the century. The social, economic, and legal position of the rich is about the same now as it was then. But the transmission of wealth by the middle class has been deeply affected by the changing nature of the family, by the desire to avoid probate, and by the sharing of the burdens of dependency and disability. Sharing the burdens of dependency and disability entails an emphasis on groups rather than individuals, and the sharing has been made possible in large part by disagreeable taxation and controversial income transfers.

The desire to share burdens is firmly fixed, and the majority are not likely to abandon that desire. Nonetheless, successful sharing requires a consensus that it is worthwhile. The day-to-day cost of sharing burdens is borne by the work force. The willingness of the work force to bear that cost turns on perceptions that cost (including that part attributable to waste and fraud) is not excessive.

Because the shift to new forms of property (principally pension benefits) occurred over a relatively short period of time, it has been characterized by variety, abuse, and disappointed expectations. Variety can be and is a source of experimentations and improvement. Abuse of property forms is a part of the history of property, but abuse can be controlled. Disappointment with the new forms of property is inevitable to the extent that expectations are unreasonable. Transmission of wealth from generation to generation on an individual basis has not proceeded altogether smoothly after a thousand years of Anglo-American experience. It is therefore hardly surprising that wealth transmission on a group basis and common ownership of some kinds of property have encountered difficulties. The difficulties are not insurmountable, but it is critical that they receive careful attention because resolution has become politicized. The law of wills, trusts, and future interests is not dead. It is being displaced to a considerable extent by new law that developed quickly and imperfectly. It already exists. The pressing task is to make it work.

Notes

1. Heilbroner, *Middle-Class Myths, Middle-Class Realities*, The Atlantic Monthly, Oct. 1976, at 37.

2. *See generally* Hacker, *Farewell to the Family?* The New York Review of Books, Mar. 18, 1982, at 37; *Saving the Family*, Newsweek, May 15, 1978, at 63; Mead, *Can the American Family Survive?*, Redbook, Feb. 1977, at 91.

3. *See* 5 Page on the Law of Wills § 47.38 (W. Bowe and D. Parker eds. 1962).

4. Employee resistance to relocation is said to be increasing. *Mobile Society Puts Down Roots*, Time, June 12, 1978, at 73.

5. Gelman, *How Marriages Can Last*, Newsweek, July 13, 1981, at 73.

6. *See generally* Hafen, *Puberty, Privacy, and Protection: The Risks of Children's "Rights,"* 63 A.B.A.J. 1383 (1977).

7. *Roe v. Wade*, 410 U.S. 113 (1973).

8. *Bellotti v. Baird*, 428 U.S. 132 (1976).

9. *See generally Working Women, Joys and Sorrows*, U.S. News & World Report, Jan. 15, 1979, at 64.

10. *See generally* Ling, *Baby-Sitting Is Big Business*, Forbes, July 24, 1978, at 80; *Making Millions by Baby-Sitting*, Time, July 3, 1978, at 65.

11. *See* C. Lasch, Haven in a Heartless World 171–178 (1977).

12. *See generally* Chapter 5 *infra,* The Employee Retirement Income Security Act (ERISA), at 85.

13. Under the doctrine of *ancestral property* (rarely a part of modern law), inherited property owned by an intestate decedent passes only to such collaterals as are of the "blood of the first purchaser." A. Casner and W. Leach, Cases and Text on Property 249 (2d ed. 1969).

14. *See,* for example, Ohio Rev. Code §§ 1339.31–1339.39.

15. 29 U.S.C. § 1055 (1975).

16. *See generally HMOs: Are They the Answer to Your Medical Needs?,* Consumer Reports, Oct. 1974, at 756.

17. *See* Giving in America 53–75 (Report, Commission on Private Philanthropy and Public Needs, 1975).

18. *See* Foundations, Private Giving and Public Policy 13–16 (Report and Recommendations of the Commission on Foundations and Private Philanthropy, 1970).

19. *See generally* Simon and Hansmann, *The Role of the Non-Profit Corporation,* Yale Alumni Magazine, Apr. 1978, at 42; Rockefeller, *The Third Sector,* Across the Board, Mar. 1978, at 13.

20. *Saving a Station: Grand Central Wins in Court,* Time, July 10, 1978, at 26.

21. *See generally* Kay, *The Recycling of Boston,* Saturday Review, Feb. 5, 1977, at 38; McQuade, *Two Cities New and Old Show the Way to Urban Amenity,* Fortune, July 1975, at 92.

22.. *See Landmarks That Work,* Newsweek, June 19, 1978, at 63.

23. *A Well-Kept Secret: Nation's 50 New Parks,* U.S. News & World Report, June 5, 1978, at 58.

24. Witness the controversy over the Alaska National Interest Lands Conservation Act. New York Times, June 19, 1978, § II, at 4, col. 1.

25. W. Defuniak & M. Vaughn, Principles of Community Property § 68 (2d ed. 1971).

26. On the Department of Health and Human Services, *see The Beneficent Monster,* Time, June 12, 1978, at 24; on Federal pay scales, *see* Bethell, *The Wealth of Washington,* Harper's, June 1978, at 41.

27. *The Tax Mess,* Newsweek, Apr. 10, 1978, at 70.

28. A. Okun, Equality and Efficiency: The Big Tradeoff 67 (1975); Theobald, *The Background to the Guaranteed Income Concept* 83, in The Guaranteed Income (R. Theobald ed. 1965–1966).

29. *See generally* A. Munnell, The Future of Social Security 25–61 (1977).

30. *See generally* Who Gets Food Stamps? 6–10 (Senate Select Committee on Nutrition and Human Needs, 94th Cong., 1st Sess., 1975).

31. *See* Edgerton, *The Tax Reform You May Need Most,* Money, June 1978, at 48.

32. Mayer, *The Graying of America,* Newsweek, Feb. 28, 1977, at 50.

33. *See* R. Tilove, Public Employee Pension Funds 168–173. (1976).

34. *See generally How Safe Is Your Pension Plan?* U.S. News & World Report, June 12, 1978, at 78; Ehrbar, *Those Pension Plans Are Even Weaker Than You Think,* Fortune, Nov. 1977, at 104.

35. Fritz, *Union Corruption, Worse than Ever,* U.S. News & World Report, Sept. 8, 1980, at 33.

36. Pension Benefit Guaranty Corporation, Contingent Employer Liability Insurance: Status Report to the Congress 10–15 (July 1, 1978).

37. *See* Main, *Building a 21st-Century Pension Right Now,* Money, Sept. 1976, at 38.

38. *Threat to an American Tradition,* Time, May 22, 1978, at 96.

39. Pub. L. No. 91–172, 83 Stat. 487 [Codified in scattered sections of 26 U.S.C. (1969)].

40. *See* W. Smith & C. Chiechi, Private Foundations Before and After the Tax Reform Act of 1969 76–82 (1974); J. Labovitz, The Impact of the Private Foundation Provisions of the Tax Reform Act of 1969: Early Empirical Measurements 77–78 (Research Contributions of the American Bar Foundation, 1974, No. 2); Bittker, *Should Foundations Be Third-Class Charities?,* in The Future of Foundations 132, 159–162 (F. Heimann, ed. 1973).

41. *See generally* M. Fremont-Smith, Foundations and Government—State and Federal Law and Supervision 272–408 (1965).

5 The Employee Retirement Income Security Act (ERISA)

ERISA—the Employee Retirement Security Act of 1974—is a federal statute regulating pension and welfare plans created by employers or employee associations (or both) engaged in interstate commerce.[1] Of the stated exceptions from the ambit of the act, two are noteworthy.[2] Government (Federal, state, and local) pension plans are excluded, as are church plans not electing coverage.

ERISA consists of four titles. Title I (the *labor* title) deals with assuring pensions to participants in plans covered by the act.[3] Title II (the *tax* title) amends the Internal Revenue Code.[4] Title III assigns responsibility for administering the act.[5] Title IV establishes the Pension Benefit Guaranty Corporation (PBGC), a nonprofit government corporation, which administers plan-termination insurance.[6]

The overall thrust of ERISA is to assure retirement income to participants in pension plans. This objective is sought through statutory provisions on (1) *early vesting* of pension rights, (2) funding of pension plans, and (3) fiduciary responsibility. These provisions on the characteristics of plans are complemented by statutory requirements on dissemination of information with respect to plans and creation of plan-termination insurance.

ERISA also created the Individual Retirement Account (IRA). IRAs were originally intended primarily for employees not covered by tax-qualified private pension plans or government pension plans, but the Economic Recovery Tax Act of 1981 (ERTA) made IRAs available to such people. The IRA competes with the Keogh plan as a means of providing pensions for the self-employed, and it facilitates portability of pension funds when a participant in a tax-qualified pension plan changes employment. Employers may use IRAs to provide pensions through a Simplified Employee Pension Plan (SEP).[7]

ERISA does not require either employers or employee associations to create pension plans. Nor does the act set the levels of pension payments made by plans falling within the coverage of the act. A plan complying with the requirements of the statute in every respect might

---

This chapter is drawn from R.J. Lynn, *Private Pensions in Perspective: Problems of the Years Ahead,* 15 GA. L. REV. 269 (1981). Copyright © by the Georgia Law Review Association, Inc. Reprinted by permission.

nonetheless pay pensions to participants that are insufficient to maintain a comfortable standard of living, even when combined with social security retirement benefits.

ERISA does not preclude the termination of pension plans. Business corporations are formed and dissolved often and fairly easily in the United States. Creation of a pension plan is a means of attracting and holding employees. Creation of pension plans is encouraged by the federal government through the income-tax deduction, exemption, exclusion, and deferral devices. Consequently, pension (and concomitant health-and-welfare) plans have been created and doubtless are still being created in a mood of optimism that has little connection with economic reality. Some pension plans will fail, and ERISA does not prevent failure. But the act does have provisions on plan termination that are intended to protect the interests of participants.

ERISA does not make private pension credits portable on change of employment (although creation of the Individual Retirement Account, the IRA, facilitates portability); and ERISA does not insist on a survivor annuity for the spouse of a participant (although ERISA does increase the likelihood that the surviving spouse will receive an annuity).

Although ERISA requires early vesting of pension rights, it does not insist on indefeasible vesting in all cases. Thus it is essential to differentiate between contributions to a plan that originate with the participant himself and contributions that originate with the employer. With respect to contributions (mandatory or voluntary) originating with the participant in a plan, immediate vesting is required.[8] With respect to contributions originating with an employer, requirements are more complex, and are described later in this discussion under "Vesting."

The Principal Features of ERISA

Preemption of State and Local Law

Section 514 (a) of ERISA states that "except as provided in subsection (b) of this section, the provisions of [Title I—the labor title] and Title IV [on plan termination and the Pension Benefit Guaranty Corporation] shall supersede any and all State laws insofar as they may now or hereafter relate to any employee benefit plan [previously] described. . . ."[9]

Subsection (b) of Section 514 provides that preemption does not apply to "generally applicable criminal law" of a state, nor to "any cause of action which arose, or any act or omission which occurred, before January 1, 1975," and that "nothing in this title shall be construed

The Employee Retirement Income Security Act 87

to exempt or relieve any person from any law of any State which regulates insurance, banking, or securities.''[10]

With respect to plans covered by ERISA, the act supersedes state and local law on vesting, fiduciary responsibility, and funding; on disclosure and reporting; and on plan termination insurance (all considered later in this discussion).

Individual Retirement Accounts (IRAs)

Under ERISA as amended from time to time since 1974,[11] an employee or a self-employed person can contribute his compensation, or $2,000, whichever is less, to an Individual Retirement Account, and treat the contribution as a deduction for federal-income-tax purposes. Falling under social security does not preclude contributing to an IRA. Income on the account is not subject to the income tax until distributions from the account occur.

Both husband and wife may be employed or self-employed, under circumstances such that each is eligible to set up an IRA. If so, each may do so, and each is entitled to the appropriate deduction for income-tax purposes. If a person eligible to set up an IRA is married to a nonemployed person, the employed or self-employed spouse may, if he wishes, contribute on behalf of the nonemployed spouse to a separate IRA for the nonemployed spouse. In such a case, the maximum annual contribution, (and income-tax deduction) is the lesser of (1) the contributor's compensation or (2) $2,250, split in any ratio between the accounts, but with no more than $2,000 to either account.

IRAs can be established through banks, savings-and-loan associations, credit unions, and mutual funds. Individual retirement annuities are sold by insurance companies. Special individual retirement bonds are issued by the United States government. Except in the cases of disability or death, distributions from an IRA before age fifty-nine and a half are subject to income-tax and a penalty tax. Distributions from the account are required to begin no later than age seventy and a half; otherwise a penalty tax is incurred. Distributions can be made in a lump sum or in the form of an annuity.

Borrowing from an IRA subjects it to income tax at ordinary income rates. Pledging the account as security for a loan is treated for tax purposes as a distribution to the extent of the pledge.

An IRA can be used to achieve a tax-free *rollover*. For example, suppose that *A* is a participant with fully vested benefits in a tax-qualified pension plan. His employment terminates, and he receives a lump-sum distribution of his benefits. *A* becomes self-employed, and sets up an

IRA. If *A* reinvests the lump-sum distribution in the IRA in accordance with the requirements of ERISA, the rollover is tax free. Similarly, although IRAs are generally nontransferable, a transfer to a former spouse under a valid divorce decree or an agreement incident to a divorce is tax free.

Vesting

Accrual of pension benefits is accumulating credits (in the case of a defined benefit plan) or accumulating funds in an individual employee pension account (in the case of a defined contribution plan). ERISA sets out permissible methods of accruing benefits. Accrual is related to vesting, but accrual of benefits and vesting of benefits are not the same. Vesting gives a nonforfeitable right to a pension at retirement age, irrespective of continuing employment. Where pension benefits are based solely on employer contributions, it is possible under ERISA for accrual of benefits to occur for some years with no vesting. In contrast, to the extent that pension benefits are based on employee contributions, ERISA requires immediate vesting.

Although the act requires early vesting of accrued benefits based on employer contributions,[12] three vesting schedules are provided for. The alternatives available are: (1) 100-percent vesting after ten years' service (with no vesting prior to ten years); (2) gradual vesting over fifteen years (25-percent vesting after five years' service, 5-percent vesting per year for the next five years, and 10-percent vesting for the last five years); and (3) the *rule of 45* (50-percent vesting where the age of a participant when added to his years of service—not less than five—equals forty-five, plus 10-percent vesting for each year thereafter). There are also special rules for pension plans favoring highly paid employees *(top-heavy plans)*.

By taking account of both the age of a participant and years of service, the rule of 45 permits earlier vesting for older participants, particularly women entering the work force later in life after having fulfilled family responsibilities.

The schedules of vesting provided for by ERISA can hardly be termed generous. Fringe benefits provided to employees by employers—including employer contributions to pension funds—are commonly regarded as forgone wages. Yet full vesting with respect to such contributions can be deferred (and is likely to be deferred) for a considerable number of years.

Service and Breaks in Service

Participation in a pension plan, accrual of pension benefits, and vesting of pension benefits presuppose employment, or *service,* as it is customarily called in this connection. For example, a plan might provide for full vesting after ten years' service. ERISA and accompanying regulations set minimum standards for ascertaining years of service and hours of service, and create rules on breaks in service that arise when employment is interrupted.[13] For purposes of participation and vesting, a year of service is usually determined by the number of hours of service credited to an employee in a period of twelve consecutive months, and a year of service is 1,000 or more hours of service in such twelve-month period. (The maritime industry, seasonal industries, and less than full-time service require separate discussion and are not considered here.) For accrual and vesting purposes, a plan may designate any period of twelve consecutive months. For participation purposes, the period must begin on employment.

There are three permissible methods for determining years of service. Under the first, hours of service are determined from records of hours worked (on the job), hours for which the employee is paid (or entitled to be paid) though not on the job (for example, during illness), and hours for which back pay is awarded or agreed to by the employer. An employee accumulating 1,000 hours of service during the applicable twelve-month period is credited with a year of service.

To avoid the detail required by the first method to determine years of service, an employer might use the *equivalency* method for determining years of service based on (1) working time, (2) periods of employment, or (3) earnings. Under an equivalency method, a specified number of hours less than 1,000 can be treated as the equivalent of 1,000. For example, if a plan credits an employee only with hours worked and he is credited with at least 870 hours, he is treated as credited with 1,000 hours—a year of service.

A third method for determining years of service is the *elapsed-time* method. Years of service are determined by considering the total time that elapses during employment under a plan, irrespective of the number of hours of service completed in any twelve-month period. For example, an employee under a multiemployer plan employed from January 1, 1976, to December 31, 1985, is credited with ten years' service.

A break in service can result, of course, from termination of employment, but it can occur for a number of other reasons: an extended sickleave, a layoff,[14] jury duty, or a call to military service.

Pension plans frequently have break-in-service rules. Denial of a pension because of breaks in service can occur under ERISA, but ERISA decreases the likelihood of such denial by creating rules on breaks in service. Plan rules cannot be more strict than those described in the act.

A plan other than one using the elapsed-time method of determining service can designate as a one-year break in service a year in which the employee has not completed more than 500 hours of service, or the equivalent of 500 hours if the plan uses the equivalency method of determining service. Interruptions of service of less than one year cannot be recognized as breaks in service. The year can be any twelve-month period designated by the plan provided the twelve-month period is applied consistently. From the fact that an employee has completed more than 500 hours of service in a year (so that there is no break in service), it does not necessarily follow that benefits will accrue for that year. Suppose that A is employed under a pension plan that requires at least 1,000 hours of service during the year as a prerequisite to accrual of benefits. A is employed for 600 hours during the year. Although he has not had a break in service, he is not entitled to accrual of benefits for the year because the plan does not provide for accrual under such circumstances and cannot be required to do so.

The effect of a break in service turns on the number of years of break compared with the number of years of service before the break, the status of the employee's accrued benefits, and the type of plan (defined-benefit plan, defined-contribution plan, or plan funded solely by insurance contracts). For example, suppose that A enters employment under a noncontributory plan providing 100-percent vesting after ten years' service (with no vesting prior to ten years). A terminates his employment after four years' service and incurs five consecutive one-year breaks in service before he returns to work covered by the plan, and accumulates six consecutive years of service. Because the aggregate number of consecutive one-year breaks in service exceeds the aggregate number of years of service preceding the break, the plan lawfully can disregard the years of prebreak service in determining ten years' service for vesting purposes.

Eligibility for Participation

Pension plans frequently impose age and service requirements as prerequisites to participation. Under ERISA, generally speaking, a plan imposing such requirements cannot postpone participation beyond the time an employee completes one year of service and attains age twenty-five, whichever occurs later.[15] For example, if A enters employment at age twenty-two and completes a year of service, a pension plan can lawfully deny him participation until he attains twenty-five. A year of service for participation purposes is a period of twelve consecutive months, beginning with the date of employment, and service is not less than 1,000 hours during such a twelve-month period for which the employee is paid or entitled to be paid. (A year of service can also be determined for participation purposes by the equivalency method, or by the elapsed-time method, as described earlier.) If a plan provides for full vesting after three years' service, participation cannot be postponed beyond the time an employee completes three years' service and attains age twenty-five, whichever occurs later. For example, if A enters employment at age thirty under a pension plan providing for full vesting after three years, the plan can deny him participation until he has three years of service. The plan of an educational institution providing for full vesting after one year of service cannot postpone participation beyond the time an employee completes one year of service or attains age thirty, whichever occurs later.

A defined-benefit plan may lawfully deny participation to an employee who begins employment at an age within five years of the normal retirement age under the plan. For example, if A, aged sixty-two, begins work with an employer sponsoring a plan with a normal retirement age of sixty-five, the plan can lawfully exclude A from participation. Defined-contribution plans cannot deny participation because of entry into employment later in life.

Eligibility for participation does not necessarily mean immediate participation. ERISA does not require that an employee be admitted to participation in a pension plan upon attaining eligibility, but the plan must admit him no later than six months after he has attained eligibility or at the beginning of the first plan year following eligibility, whichever occurs first.

The Surviving Spouse under ERISA

A criticism frequently leveled at some pension systems is that a surviving spouse of a participant cannot receive a pension under the system (because the system makes no provision at all for a surviving spouse), or that a surviving spouse who might receive a pension under the system has little assurance of receiving one (because the mechanics of the system are geared to *exclusion* of the spouse as beneficiary).[16] There are, of course, notable exceptions. Although social security was, until comparatively recently, rife with sex bias, it did and does include provision for a surviving spouse (and, indeed, for a surviving divorced spouse).

ERISA does not assure a pension to the surviving spouse of a participant. Rather, the act increases the probability that a surviving spouse will qualify for a pension. It does so through two requirements.[17] First, most pension plans providing retirement annuities must now also offer a *joint and survivor annuity,* that is, an annuity payable to the participant for life and then to his or her surviving spouse if any. Second, generally speaking, under ERISA, retirement benefits taken in the form of an annuity (rather than, say, a lump-sum distribution) are taken automatically in the form of a joint and survivor annuity unless the participant rejects that form of annuity in writing.

The required joint and survivor annuity must be not less than the actuarial equivalent of an annuity for the life of the participant alone. The survivor annuity for the spouse of the participant must be not less than one-half the amount payable during the joint lives of the participant and his spouse nor greater than that amount.

If an employee continues to work after he is eligible for early retirement (at, say, age sixty), and at a time when his pension plan must offer a joint and survivor annuity, election of a survivor annuity by the participant is not necessarily automatic during the period between his eligibility for early retirement and his eligibility for normal retirement (at, say, age sixty-five). Rather, a plan might lawfully require that the participant elect the survivor annuity in writing to assure a pension to his surviving spouse should he die before retiring.

Portability of Pension Rights

Vested rights of a participant in a pension plan under ERISA are not portable in the way that the quarters of coverage of an insured under social security are transferable on change from one covered employment to another. Rather, ERISA facilitates portability by permitting a tax-free rollover of funds from the tax-qualified pension plan of one employer to the tax-qualified pension plan of another employer, or to an Individual Retirement Account.[18] For example, suppose that *A,* a participant in a qualified pension plan, has vested rights in the plan. *A*'s employment is terminated, and *A* is paid a lump-sum distribution by the plan. In accordance with the requirements of ERISA, *A* reinvests the distribution in the qualified plan of his new employer. If *A* does not find new employment promptly, *A* reinvests the distribution in an Individual Retirement Account. The Individual Retirement Account can act as a conduit for the distribution from the qualified plan of one employer to the qualified plan of another employer. A lump-sum distribution that is rolled over into an Individual Retirement Account is, of course, subject to the rules regulating Individual Retirement Accounts. (For example, an excise tax is levied on a premature withdrawal from the account.)

Fiduciary Responsibility

ERISA tries to assure a regular flow of pension benefits to participants and beneficiaries by identifying fiduciaries, imposing standards of fiduciary conduct, and simply prohibiting some kinds of transactions.[19] Under ERISA, a *fiduciary* is anyone who (1) exercises any discretionary authority or discretional control respecting management of a plan, or exercises any authority or control respecting management or disposition of plan assets; (2) renders investment advice for a fee or other compensation (direct or indirect) with respect to any monies or other property of a plan, or has any authority or responsibility to do so; or (3) has any discretionary authority or discretionary responsibility in the administration of a plan. These definitions of "fiduciary" cut a wider swath than the customary definition, namely, one who holds and manages property that belongs wholly or partially to persons other than himself. Included among fiduciaries then are plan trustees and officers and members of the plan's investment committee. ERISA requires that a fiduciary discharge his duties solely in the interest of participants and beneficiaries and for the exclusive purpose of providing benefits and defraying reasonable expenses of administration.

The act adopts the *prudent-man rule,* which requires a fiduciary to discharge his duties with respect to a plan with the care, skill, prudence, and diligence, under the circumstances then prevailing, that a prudent man acting in a like capacity and familiar with such matters would use in the conduct of an enterprise of a like character and with like aims. Except for eligible individual account plans, diversification of investments is required (unless imprudent) to minimize the risk of large losses.

Specified kinds of transactions between a plan and a party in interest are prohibited. A *party in interest* is (1) any fiduciary (including but not limited to any administrator, officer, trustee, or custodian), counsel, or employee of a plan; (2) a person providing services to a plan; (3) an employer of covered employees; (4) an employee organization whose members are covered; (5) an owner (direct or indirect) of 50 percent or more of the company; (6) certain relatives of parties in interest; or (7) certain other related businesses or persons. A *relative* is defined as a spouse, ancestor, lineal descendant, or spouse of a lineal descendant.

Prohibited transactions between a plan and a party in interest include direct or indirect sale, exchange, or lease of property; lending money or extension of credit; and furnishing goods, services, or facilities. Transfer of plan assets to, or use by or for the benefit of, a party in interest is forbidden. Except for certain kinds of plans, such as profit sharing or employee stock ownership, investment of more than 10 percent of plan assets in employer securities or employer real property is prohibited.

To avoid conflict of interest and self-dealing, a fiduciary is expressly prohibited from (1) dealing with the assets of a plan in his own interest or for his own account; (2) acting individually or in any other capacity, in any transaction involving a plan, on behalf of a party whose interests are adverse to the interests of the plan, its participants, or beneficiaries; or (3) receiving any consideration for his own personal account from any party dealing with a plan in connection with a transaction involving plan assets.

There are some exemptions from prohibited transactions. For example, if no more than reasonable compensation is paid, arrangements with a party in interest for legal, accounting, or other necessary services for a plan are permissible.

Bonding of people who handle plan funds or property is usually required. People convicted of certain crimes are prohibited for a stipulated period of time from serving in specified positions with respect to plans.

Consistent with traditional law on fiduciary administration, a fiduciary who fails in his duty is personally liable for any loss resulting from his failure, and under specified circumstances, he is responsible for breach of fiduciary duty by a cofiduciary. For example, a fiduciary is held responsible if he conceals an act or omission of another fiduciary, knowing such act or omission to be a breach of duty.

Funding

Two common kinds of private pension plans are defined-benefit plans and defined-contribution (or money-purchase) plans. A defined-benefit plan specifies the pension payable (for example, a flat sum per month at retirement) or specifies the method of calculating the pension payable but does not specify the amount set aside periodically (the contribution) required to fund the pension. A defined-contribution plan specifies the amount set aside to fund the pension, but not the pension payable (the pension payable will turn on accumulated contributions and investment yield on accumulated contributions). Pension plans have tended to be defined-benefit plans rather than defined-contribution plans.

Whether a pension plan is of the defined-benefit type or the defined-contribution type, the pension payable depends on both regular funding and investment experience. ERISA attempts to assure the fiscal integrity of plans falling within its ambit by requiring adequate funding and by penalizing underfunding through imposition of an excise tax on the accumulated funding deficiency.[20] Before ERISA, funding of defined-benefit plans might not be sufficient to amortize past service liabilities. *Past service liabilities* are the costs of providing pensions to employees for past service for which no contributions were made.

With respect to defined-benefit plans, ERISA requires that the employer's periodic contribution include not only normal costs—those incident to meeting pension liabilities as they accrue—but also sums sufficient to amortize past service costs and experience losses.[21] Past service costs for plans in existence at the effective date of ERISA must be amortized in equal installments over forty years. Past service costs for new plans must be amortized in equal installments over thirty years.

With respect to money-purchase plans, the funding requirements of ERISA are met if the employer makes the contribution called for by the plan. The new funding rules of ERISA do not apply to profit-sharing plans, stock-bonus plans, and some insured-pension plans. Because the impact of the new funding rules falls most heavily on defined-benefit plans, sponsors of new pension plans might be less likely to adopt defined-benefit plans.

Disclosure and Reporting

ERISA requires that plan administrators disclose to participants information on plans and that administrators report on a regular basis to the federal government (the Department of Labor, the Internal Revenue Service, and the Pension Benefit Guaranty Corporation).[22] Because disclosure and reporting requirements are inevitably criticized as burdensome, they will be changed in the light of experience. Therefore the detail on such requirements is much less important than either the arguments for imposing requirements or the general thrust of the requirements.

The assumption underlying disclosure to participants is that an informed participant will protect his interest in a plan. The assumption underlying reporting requirements is that enforcement of the law by government requires a continual flow of information on plans. One cannot fault either of these assumptions as irrational, but it is unwise to put full faith in either.

Participation in a pension plan is of immediate interest to the elderly, the disabled, and those about to leave the work force permanently, either voluntarily or involuntarily. Retirement is remote, however, to an employee in his twenties or thirties. A cut in his paycheck brings from him an immediate response, but investment of pension funds is, for him, academic. Even the most carefully prepared information given to him on his pension plan may therefore not be read.

Similarly, a regular flow of information on pensions to the Department of Labor, the Internal Revenue Service, and the Pension Benefit

Guaranty Corporation can assist in securing to participants in plans and to their beneficiaries the benefits to which they are entitled. But from the fact that information is available, it does not follow that it will be examined carefully and used judiciously. Enforcement requires both a staff to enforce and a desire to enforce. Both will vary from time to time.

Some information available to participants or beneficiaries receiving benefits is furnished as a matter of course (for example, the summary plan description). Some is furnished on written request (for example, a statement of total benefits accrued). For some kinds of information, a reasonable charge can be made (for example, the documents under which the plan is operated). Some kinds of information must be made available at, say, the principal office of the administrator (for example, the bargaining agreement establishing the plan). Certain kinds of information on plans assembled by the Department of Labor and the Treasury Department are open to public inspection at designated locations.

The Pension Benefit Guaranty Corporation

ERISA created the Pension Benefit Guaranty Corporation (PBGC), a nonprofit corporation within the Department of Labor, to administer an insurance program.[23] The PBGC collects insurance premiums (generally at a stated sum per participant), maintains trust funds, and insures the vested pension benefits (within set limits) of participants and beneficiaries of defined-benefit pension plans. Defined-contribution pension plans do not fall within the purview of the PBGC because they do not promise a specified benefit.

On termination of a pension plan, benefits are assured as far as possible from pension-fund assets; thereafter, before turning to the PBGC insurance trust fund to meet pension liabilities, the PBGC may resort to a limited portion of the assets of the employer (contingent liability).[24] *Contingent employer liability* is to be differentiated from employer-withdrawal liability under the Multiemployer Pension Plan Amendments Act of 1980. With some exceptions, the employer's entire assets are subject to employer-withdrawal liability.

The PBGC is administered by a board of directors consisting of the secretary of labor (chairman), the secretary of the treasury, and the secretary of commerce. At the close of each fiscal year, the PBGC must report to the president and Congress. The report must include information on the insurance trust funds maintained by the PBGC.

Because ERISA was hailed as inaugurating a new era of assured pension benefits, the limited impact of the PBGC bears emphasis. For example, pension plans of state and local governments are outside the ambit of ERISA and are therefore not insured by the PBGC. Church plans are not covered by ERISA unless they elect coverage. Money-purchase pension plans, profit-sharing plans, and stock-bonus plans cannot be insured. In short, the PBGC offers assurance that pension benefits, within specified limits, will be paid to participants and beneficiaries of insured pension plans. Not all plans, by any means, are insured.

Contingent Employer-Liability Insurance

On pension-plan termination, if pension-fund assets are insufficient to pay guaranteed benefits, Section 4062 of ERISA imposes limited liability for the deficiency on the employer.[25] Liability is equal to the lesser of (1) the amount of the deficiency, or (2) 30 percent of the employer's net worth as of a day chosen by the Pension Benefit Guaranty Corporation but not more than 120 days prior to the date of termination, computed without regard to any liability under Title IV of the act. Section 4023 of ERISA directs the Pension Benefit Guaranty Corporation to "insure any employer . . . against the payment of any [contingent] liability imposed on him" by the act.[26] The desirability of providing such contingent employer-liability insurance has been questioned by the Pension Benefit Guaranty Corporation itself, and such insurance does not exist.[27]

Private Pension Problems of the 1980s

Some of the private pension problems of the 1980s—fiscal integrity, certainty of benefits, and portability of rights—are not remarkably different from the problems of twenty-five years ago.[28] ERISA addressed these problems, but clearly did not altogether solve them. Persisting pension problems have been accentuated and the number of problems increased by demographic change,[29] rising expectations, changes in the family,[30] changes in the role of women, inflation,[31] sluggish capital formation,[32] and declining productivity.[33] In short, pension problems reflect social and economic change, and where change is unexpected or generally damaging, the jolt to all pension systems is often severe. To private pension plans, a jolt could be catastrophic.[34]

Inflation

Although many important support benefits (for example, medical care and housing) are payable in kind, pensions are payable in money. Inflation affects both payments in kind and payments in money because a dollar that today buys less than it did in the past buys fewer goods and services that are the goal of all support systems—public, quasi-public, and purely private—irrespective of whether payment is in kind or in money or in a mix of both. Nonetheless, the eroding effects of inflation on support benefits usually are associated with benefits payable in money.

When pensions are unfunded and are payable from general tax revenues, a decline in the purchasing power of the pension dollar can be offset by simply increasing the amount of the pension. Indeed, such increases occur with regularity, particularly when pension beneficiaries are organized and politically active. But unlike public pension plans, particularly federal plans, private pension plans rarely index benefits to reflect changes in the value of money.

This state of affairs is not inevitable. When pensions are funded, as private pensions are, inflation can be anticipated and a rate of inflation factored into the actuarial assumptions that underlie periodic contributions to accumulated pension funds. If the actuarial assumption for inflation anticipates increased benefits not only for those participants still employed but also for those already retired, pensions paid can be increased periodically to offset decline in the purchasing power of the pension benefit. Increasing pensions paid to retired participants assumes a willingness on the part of the work force to pay for the increased benefit (just as blanketing in groups not covered by pension plans or covered by inadequate plans assumes a willingness by participants in the absorbing plan to bear the cost of absorption). When the rate of inflation is moderate, periodic adjustment of benefits payable is politically feasible.

The rub is that the rate of inflation is unpredictable.[35] All support systems are part of the money-exchange system. The disastrous effects of a moderate rate of inflation on the third sector are already being documented.[36] If inflation overwhelms the exchange system, private pensions will fail, and the Pension Benefit Guaranty Corporation cannot save them. A consequence might well be the absorption of all pension systems into the social security system. If that occurs, the problem of portability of private-pension credits finally will be solved.

Compulsory Retirement

Assumptions underlying pension systems include the possibility that some participants eligible for benefits will retire early (before the customary age of sixty-five) and that every participant eligible for retirement will retire at some predetermined age (frequently as high as age seventy).

When pensions are funded, such features of the pension structure are factors considered in calculating periodic additions to the trust fund.

Compulsory retirement is undergoing reexamination in the United States.[37] Congress has addressed the matter,[38] but congressional action does not foreclose further controversy. There is little reason to think that in the decade ahead private pensions will escape embroilment in the issue. Like the issue of pension differences based on sex,[39] the issue of compulsory retirement has economic, social,[40] and political aspects.[41] Although contemporary discussions of mandatory retirement tend to emphasize freedom to work, irrespective of age, as long as one is capable of doing so, the issue is much more complicated than that. As the proportion of aged and retired people in the population increases, it will be increasingly burdensome for the work force to support them.[42] The elderly might indeed insist on working as long as they are capable of doing so (it is not unthinkable that both the day laborer and the Supreme Court justice are at some time disabled by age from working). But the insistence of the elderly that they be *permitted* to work if they choose might be buttressed by an insistence by the work force that all who can *must* support themselves, irrespective of age, if capable of doing so.

Ideally, we should avoid absolutes in this connection and seek flexibility. We might try to accommodate both optional early retirement and an optional working life of indefinite duration, on the one hand (when they do not bear too heavily on the work force and on the young seeking to enter the work force), and automatic retirement (at some normal retirement age), on the other. Automatic retirement at normal retirement age might be the general rule, but the general rule should be complemented by another rule entitling the employee to seek a waiver of the general rule, with the burden on the employer to show that the waiver should not be granted. Further, we should consider involuntarily retiring the old in exceptional circumstances to make way for the young when the number of positions available is limited and the pain of terminating the long and fulfilling career of the old employee is less than the pain of deferring indefinitely the career of the new.[43] (If there is a right to continue working,[44] why not a right to enter the work force?) Achieving this kind of flexibility would be difficult, but we admit persons to the work force individually, at various ages, and it is not beyond our competence to create an equitable system for leaving the work force on an individual basis.

Disability Pensions

The share of social security expenditures required to support disability pensions has drawn attention to what disability is, the feasibility of continuing current definitions of disability, and the means of avoiding abuses in a part of the income-maintenance system that does not receive the fairly regular scrutiny given to old-age pensions. Leaving the work force because of disability is different from leaving the work force because of chronological aging in that age is a matter of elapsed time. Disability, and the extent of disability, are not always so readily determined. Furthermore, we treat advanced age as disqualifying one from work of any kind. Disability might disqualify one for work of a particular kind, but it does not always disqualify one for all work. Not all who are disabled are totally and permanently disabled.[45]

Some are labeled "disabled" virtually from birth and do not enter the work force at all or are granted entry only grudgingly. That is, the so-called handicapped consist in part of those who have known disability throughout life and in part of those who have become disabled through misfortune.[46] Like other disadvantaged groups, the handicapped are organizing and are insisting on inclusion in the mainstream of life, including the world of work.

Even if the disabled were willing to be shunted aside, it is neither in their interest nor in the interest of their able-bodied counterparts that they remain outside the work force if it is at all feasible to include them. We are emerging from a period of growth and prosperity that might not be replicated for some time. We have been able to afford waste on an unparalleled scale, including waste of talent and skill. We can no longer afford unlimited waste, and there is no reason to think that a work force that perceives its self-interest will support unreasonably large numbers of people who can be trained to support themselves. In short, just as chronological age in itself might no longer justify leaving the work force, so too disability, whether congenital or acquired, might no longer justify failure to enter the work force, on the one hand, or failure to reenter the work force (after a period of disability), on the other.

A private pension plan providing disability pensions similar to those of social security and other public pension systems shares the problems associated with disability pensions, including the possibility that providing such pensions under current rules might become too burdensome. The solution to excessive cost, of course, is to grant disability pensions sparingly, when all reasonable attempts to keep the disabled in the work force have failed. Providing pensions for disability only as a last resort requires intensive effort at rehabilitation, reeducation, and retraining, but the effort will have a benefit apart from reducing pension costs—it will complement the political effort to get congenitally disabled people into the work force and will diminish the bitterness of those disabled on the job who feel dispossessed when deprived of work.

The Employee Retirement Income Security Act 101

Equality for Women

Pensions have been developed in the United States on the assumption that the participant was a male, the head of a household consisting of a wife and several dependents, and that in the normal course of events he would complete a lifetime of service with the same employer, retire, and die leaving a surviving spouse. The role of the spouse in the pension plan (if, indeed, the spouse figured in the plan at all) was clearly subordinate and derivative.

The assumption underlying the traditional view of the participant had little to recommend it,[47] but in any event, the role of women has changed significantly in just three decades, and that change affects pensions in a number of ways.

First, as members of the work force, women are participants in pension systems in their own right. They are frequently heads of households, with responsibilities identical to those of men. As fullfledged participants, they demand (and are very slowly achieving) equality of treatment with respect to both pension burdens and pension benefits.

Nonetheless, the equality women seek remains elusive.[48] Many women are not in the work force on a continuing basis. Women frequently fall under a pension plan briefly but then marry and discontinue employment (with loss of inchoate pension credits). They reenter the work force at a later time after termination of marriage by divorce or death or after children enter school. This pattern may repeat itself over a lifetime. Even where a woman's employment is fairly continuous, it might be only part-time, resulting in no accumulation of pension credits, or resulting in pension benefits payable at a minimal level. Furthermore, women continue to be excluded from the well-paid positions that conventionally lead to higher pension benefits. The social security system, for all its social-insurance ramifications, bears this earmark of the conventional pension plan—disability and retirement benefits reflect wage scales.

Another aspect of the women's-rights movement affecting pensions is the emerging insistence of women that, as spouses of participants in pension plans, they accumulate pension rights during marriage. This insistence is most evident in community-property states, but it is not (and should not be) confined to such states. This insistence raises questions regarding the application and effectiveness of *spendthrift* clauses of pension plans, and regarding the preemption of state law by ERISA.[49]

Double-Dipping and Offsets

A participant's drawing disability or retirement benefits from more than one source (particularly a tax-supported source) arouses envy and re-sentiment in other participants and their families and reinforces disillusionment in taxpayers convinced that tax dollars are spent inefficiently. Double-dipping invites the imposition of controls on drawing benefits from multiple sources. Imposing controls assumes the propriety of doing so, and propriety is not always self-evident.

For example, under 1977 amendments to the social security act, a *spouse's* retirement benefits under social security will be denied to the extent that the spouse is drawing retirement benefits from another public pension system based on the spouse's own work record.[50] Suppose that *A*, married to *B* and covered by social security, retires at age sixty-two in 1989. *B,* covered by a state retirement system, also retires at age sixty-two in 1989. To the extent that *B* receives state retirement benefits, *B*'s social security benefits as a spouse (wife, widow, husband, widower, or mother) are reduced dollar for dollar.

This automatic reduction of benefits is indefensible. First, it ignores the essential characteristic of nearly all pension systems in the 1980s. Whether public (like social security) or quasi-public (like private pensions), they are part of the income-transfer system supported by the work force. In principle, any ceiling set on disability benefits or retirement benefits should originate in what the beneficiary's earned income was and an assessment of what the work force can afford to provide willingly to nonproductive segments of the population. Second, this crude dollar-for-dollar reduction of benefits disproportionately affects groups in the work force that have long been objects of both overt and subtle discrimination—women and minorities. Women and minorities in the work force are less likely than their coworkers to be in the work force for substantial periods of time, and they are less likely to fall within the higher wage brackets. Therefore, the disability or pension benefits they receive based on their own work records are more likely to be comparatively low or minimal. Automatically denying them spouse's benefits under social security will simply exacerbate their income difficulties in many instances.

In short, the 1977 amendments to the social security act represent the worst possible manifestation of the eminently sensible effort to control support payments. A rational system for controlling double-dipping requires viewing the complete array of pension systems, identifying those systems most clearly supported by the work force, setting a ceiling on total benefits receivable that originate with the work force, and only then making adjustments in payout. Anything less works quixotically and unjustly.

The sporadic calls for a redistribution of wealth that have issued since the creation of the great American private fortunes have not been a part of the social and political history of the last three decades. Instead, there has been a demand for creation and extension of an adequate support (that is, income-maintenance) system, and as a consequence, we have been engaged in a slowly accelerating redistribution of income in the United States, bottomed principally on the federal income tax. Although there exists neither a guaranteed annual income nor a negative income tax that is so denominated, there is the equivalent in an income floor created from the various elements of the chaotic support system.

Although we tend to associate being in the work force or having been in the work force with qualifying to receive this income floor, it is important to remember that some people seeking the income floor need not themselves have worked (and, indeed, some people capable of working might never have worked and might have a fixed disinclination to work). Nonetheless, the income floor historically is an earned-income replacement or partial replacement. That being so, we can attempt to put the income floor in proper perspective.

Because the income floor is intended to replace preretirement, *earned* income, we should identify those elements of the floor that originate in the income-transfer system, for to the extent that we succeed in that task, we can arrive at a ceiling on the total payments one may receive lawfully from the support system. The work force can be reasonably asked to support a retired or disabled person in a manner approximating that which he enjoyed prior to retirement or disability, but it is foolish to assume that an informed work force will tolerate support payments (earned-income replacement) that exceed preretirement, earned income. An index (but not the sole index) to whether an element of the support system originates in the income-transfer system is to look to see whether the source of payment is the tax dollar.

To the extent that support payments originate in income transfers, we can justifiably insist on *offsetting,* that is, reducing the amount of an element or elements making up a beneficiary's total benefits, or altogether withholding an element or elements, to preclude exceeding earned income. In short, we can justifiably insist that replacement income provided by the work force not exceed preretirement, earned income.

Portability of Pension Credits

Although the Individual Retirement Account created by the Pension Reform Act of 1974 facilitates portability of private pension credits, it is highly unlikely that portability will become characteristic of private pension plans in the 1980s. Variations in funding and in vesting from plan to plan are in themselves sufficient to discourage plan sponsors from encouraging transfers of credits, to say nothing of the additional paperwork required to effect them. Consequently, significant numbers of participants drawing private pension benefits originating in disability or retirement might draw from more than one source. Where participation in more than one private pension plan is traceable to involuntary changes in employment, drawing benefits from more than one plan cannot fairly be described as double-dipping, as that expression is customarily used. Nonetheless, the practice does carry with it a duplicate servicing of but one support claim that is fragmented because of the haphazard way in which our entire support system developed. A means of avoiding such duplicate service costs is not readily apparent.

Investments

In the years after the enactment of the Pension Reform Act of 1974, both academic and business commentators puzzled over the incorporation into federal law of the prudent-man rule on trust investments, determining how the rule set out in ERISA differs from the rule of *Harvard College v. Amory*.[51] In the 1980s the focus of discussion is likely to shift dramatically. Accumulated pension funds are viewed by pension administrators as outlays.[52] To outsiders—governments, industries, unions, organized crime[53]—pension funds are sources of capital. Investing trust funds in a failing business is a breach of trust under the traditional prudent-man rule. Do employee-participants in a private pension fund have a persuasive case for abandoning traditional criteria on investment policy when their pension fund is realistically the only source of the capital required to save the business in which they are employed? Can unions representing participants in a multiemployer pension plan effectively insist that pension funds be invested to further the business objectives of the employers sponsoring the plan? Can unions effectively insist that funds be invested to further unionization?[54] Questions of this kind arising in connection with investment of private pension funds are paralleled by similar questions arising in connection with public pension plans. For example, should funds of state or municipal pension plans be invested to encourage the location of industry within a city, state, or region?[55]

When accumulated pension funds were but an obscure segment of investment capital, questions such as these rarely received attention, and clearly did not receive careful scrutiny. Private pension funds are now the most significant of the ''institutional investors,'' and participants in pension plans are slowly becoming aware of their stake in investment policy. Working out acceptable answers to questions on investments will not be easy, but development of an acceptable policy on pension-fund investment unquestionably will be a part of the evolution of pensions in the decade ahead.[56]

Conclusion

The enactment of ERISA was accompanied by much fanfare. ERISA is an important statute, but its limitations bear emphasis.

ERISA is simply a regulatory act. ERISA neither requires the creation of private pension plans nor insists that existing plans provide a minimum retirement benefit comparable to that provided to some beneficiaries under social security. Although ERISA requires the immediate vesting of any contribution to a pension plan made by the employee himself, the statute permits deferral of vesting for ten years. ERISA, through Individual Retirement Accounts (IRAs), facilitates the portability of pension credits, but it falls far short of insisting on the portability of coverage that characterizes social security. The statute gives a passing nod to the surviving spouse of a participant, but it does not assure a pension to the surviving spouse. ERISA does not preclude the termination of a pension plan. In sum, the provisions of ERISA reflect the shortcomings of the private pension device and the controversy and compromise surrounding enactment of the statute.

Proliferation of private pension plans occurred over a very short time span. Plans were created to induce prospective employees to take employment and to persuade people on the job to remain there. Private pension plans were used in the collective-bargaining process to demonstrate concern by management, on the one hand, and power by union leaders, on the other. It is hardly surprising that under these circumstances the primary purpose of the pension device—to assure a competence to a participant withdrawing from the work force because of age or disability—was lost sight of. ERISA sought to create some order and fairness in the operation of a much-abused device, and it has had some success. Some of the deficiencies of ERISA are traceable to our disinclination to consider pensions as a part of the support or income-maintenance system. If we succeed in getting a better perspective on the entire range of pension systems, public and quasi-public, we will be in a better position to amend ERISA and to improve private pension plans.

Notes

1. 29 U.S.C. §§ 1001–1381 (Supp. 1982).
2. 29 U.S.C. § 1003 (1975).
3. 29 U.S.C. §§ 1101–1144 (Supp. 1982).
4. 26 U.S.C. §§ 401–420 (Supp. 1982).
5. 29 U.S.C. §§ 1201–1204 (Supp. 1982).

6. 29 U.S.C. §§ 1301–1461 (Supp. 1982), *amending* U.S.C. §§ 1301–1381 (1975).

7. The SEP originated in section 152 of the Revenue Act of 1978, 26 U.S.C. §§ 219(b)(7), 408(k) (Supp. 1982), *amending* 26 U.S.C. §§ 219, 408 (1978).

8. 29 U.S.C. § 1053 (Supp. 1982), 26 U.S.C. § 411 (Supp. 1982).

9. 29 U.S.C. § 1144(a) (1975).

10. 29 U.S.C. § 1144(b) (1975).

11. 26 U.S.C. §§ 219, 408 (Supp. 1982), *amending* 26 U.S.C. §§ 219, 408 (1978), and related sections of the Internal Revenue Code.

12. 29 U.S.C. §§ 1053, 1054 (Supp. 1982), 26 U.S.C. § 411 (Supp. 1982).

13. 29 U.S.C. § 1052 (1975), 26 U.S.C. § 410 (Supp. 1982).

14. A *break in service*—an interruption of employment—can have tragic consequences. John Daniel worked as a truck driver from 1950 to 1973, when he retired. He joined the Teamsters Union in 1951. In 1954 a compulsory, noncontributory pension plan was adopted. Under the plan, twenty years' continuous service was a prerequisite to qualifying for a pension. Daniel received credit for five years of service at the inception of the plan because of prior work experience. He was laid off from December 1960, until April 1961. Because of embezzlement by his employer's bookkeeper, no contributions were made on his behalf between April and July 1961. Daniel could have maintained his service eligibility during those two periods by making contributions to the pension fund on his own behalf, but he did not do so. When Daniel applied for a pension upon retirement, a pension was denied him because of the break in service between December 1960, and July 1961. Daniel's subsequent unsuccessful attempt to have his interest in the pension plan denominated an "investment contract" within the meaning of the Securities Act and the Securities and Exchange Act is recounted in an opinion from the U.S. Supreme Court, *International Brotherhood of Teamsters, Chauffeurs, Warehousemen & Helpers of America v. Daniel*, 439 U.S. 551 (1979).

15. 29 U.S.C. § 1052 (1975); 26 U.S.C. § 410 (Supp. 1982).

16. *See generally* M. Meyer, Women and Employee Benefits 9–14 (1978).

17. 29 U.S.C. § 1055 (1975), 26 U.S.C. § 401 (Supp. 1982).

18. 26 U.S.C. §§ 219, 402, 403 (Supp. 1982).

19. 29 U.S.C. §§ 1101–1114 (Supp. 1982), 26 U.S.C. § 4975 (Supp. 1982).

20. 29 U.S.C. §§ 1081–1086 (Supp. 1982), 26 U.S.C. §§ 412, 4971 (Supp. 1982).

21. *See generally* Faltermayer, *A Steeper Climb Up Pension Mountain*, Fortune, Jan. 1975, at 78.

22. 29 U.S.C. §§ 1021–1031 (Supp. 1982).

23. 29 U.S.C. §§ 1301–1381 (Supp. 1982).

24. Because it might be advantageous to an employer to give up 30 percent of net assets rather than to pay an unfunded-pension liability, a Senate labor subcommittee is considering requiring a 100-percent payoff by an employer over a fifteen-year period. Brophy, *Scaring the Pensioners,* Forbes, June 21, 1982, at 32.

25. 29 U.S.C. § 1362 (Supp. 1982), *amending* 29 U.S.C. § 1362 (1975).

26. 29 U.S.C. § 1323 (Supp. 1982).

27. *See generally* Lind, *Alternatives to CELI: Strengthening and Preserving the U.S. Private Pension System,* 29 Lab. L. J. 747 (1978).

28. *See generally* Lynn, Foreman, & Wehr, *The New Inheritance: Employee Benefit Plans As a Wealth Devolution Device,* 11 Stan. L. Rev. 242 (1959).

29. *See generally* Guzzardi, *Demography's Good News for the Eighties,* Fortune, Nov. 5, 1979, at 92; Mayer, *The Graying of America,* Newsweek, Feb. 28, 1977, at 50.

30. *See generally* Hacker, *Farewell to the Family?,* The New York Review of Books, Mar. 18, 1982, at 37; Kiechel, *Two-Income Families Will Reshape the Consumer Markets,* Fortune, Mar. 10, 1980, at 110; *Our New Elite—for Better or for Worse?,* U.S. News & World Report, Feb. 25, 1980, at 65; *Saving the Family,* Newsweek, May 15, 1978, at 63; *How Men Are Changing,* Newsweek, Jan. 16, 1978, at 52.

31. *See generally* London, *Inflationary Secrets,* The New Republic, Mar. 28, 1981, at 8; Heilbroner, *The Inflation in Your Future,* The New York Review of Books, May 1, 1980, at 6; Blumberg, *White-Collar Status Panic,* The New Republic, Dec. 1, 1979, at 21.

32. *See generally* Carson-Parker, *The Capital Cloud Over Smokestack America,* Fortune, Feb. 23, 1981, at 70; Sloan & Miles, *Showdown at Capital Gap,* Forbes, Jan. 7, 1980, at 38.

33. *See generally* Bruce-Briggs, *The Dangerous Folly Called Theory Z,* Fortune, May 17, 1982, at 41; Burck, *Can Detroit Catch Up?,* Fortune, Feb. 8, 1982, at 34; Thurow, *Death by a Thousand Cuts,* The New York Review of Books, Dec. 17, 1981, at 3; Burck, *What's in It for the Unions?,* Fortune, Aug. 24, 1981, at 88; Burck, *What Happens When Workers Manage Themselves,* Fortune, July 27, 1981, at 62; Lubar, *Rediscovering the Factory,* Fortune, July 13, 1981, at 52; Burck, *Working Smarter,* Fortune, June 15, 1981, at 68.

34. *See generally Danger: Pension Perils Ahead,* Time, Sept. 24, 1979, at 68; *The Pension Mess,* Newsweek, Feb. 26, 1979, at 67; Ehrbar, *Those Pension Plans Are Even Weaker Than You Think,* Fortune, Nov. 1977, at 104.

35. Committee for Economic Development, Fighting Inflation and Promoting Growth 11–20 (1976).

36. W. Nielsen, The Endangered Sector 8–13 (1979).

37. *See generally* Trippett, *Looking Askance at Ageism,* Time, Mar. 24, 1980, at 88; *Now, the Revolt of the Old,* Time, Oct. 10, 1977, at 18; Seixas, *Time to Rethink Compulsory Retirement,* Money, Apr. 1977, at 42.

38. Congress in 1978 amended the Age Discrimination in Employment Act to raise the legal mandatory-retirement age for most working Americans from sixty-five to seventy. 29 U.S.C. § 631 (Supp. 1982), *amending* 29 U.S.C. § 631 (1975). The ADEA states that "no . . . employee benefit plan shall require or permit the involuntary retirement of any individual . . . because of the age of such individual." 29 U.S.C. § 623 (Supp. 1982), *amending* 29 U.S.C. § 623 (1975).

39. Fields, *TIAA-CREF to Defer 'Unisex' Pensions until Court Resolves 2 Lawsuits,* The Chronicle of Higher Education, May 12, 1982, at 1, cols. 2–4; Fields, *'Unisex Table' for Pensions Stirs Questions,* The Chronicle of Higher Education, May 5, 1980, at 1, col. 4. In *City of Los Angeles, Department of Power and Water v. Manhart,* 435 U.S. 702 (1978), the Supreme Court held that under Title VII of the Civil Rights Act of 1964 and the Equal Pay Act of 1963, it is unlawful to require female employees to make larger pension-fund contributions than those required of male employees to receive the same monthly benefit on retirement.

40. H. Maurer, *Older Professionals: "Sic Transit Gloria Mundi,"* in Not Working 221 (1979).

41. *See generally* Ross, *Retirement at Seventy: A New Trauma for Management,* Fortune, May 8, 1978, at 106.

42. In this connection, immigration of the young into the United States might help to alleviate the problem. *See generally* Berman, *Does the Melting Pot Still Meld,* Forbes, Oct. 30, 1978, at 63; Wachter, *Second Thoughts About Illegal Immigrants,* Fortune, May 22, 1978, at 80.

43. Scharff, *Will Delayed Retirements Put Your Promotion on Hold?,* Money, May 1978, at 93.

44. *See generally* Gilder, *The Make-Work Economy,* Harper's, Nov. 1979, at 39.

45. In the *State, ex rel. Consolidation Coal Co. v. Industrial Commission of Ohio,* 62 Ohio St. 2d 147, 404 N.E.2d 141 (1980), the Supreme Court of Ohio concluded that a claimant of workers' compensation was not precluded from pursuing a claim for permanent *partial* disability originating in an alleged back injury by the fact that he had already been found to be permanently and *totally* disabled as a result of coal miner's pneumoconiosis.

46. *See generally* Gliedman & Roth, *The Unexpected Minority,* The New Republic, Feb. 2, 1980, at 26.

47. In particular, the assumption ignores the proclivity of a signif-

icant number of people to change jobs from time to time. In the absence of early vesting of pension credits and portability of pension credits, frequent changes in employment either preclude qualifying for a pension or require qualifying for a pension originating in several sources.

48. *See generally The Superwoman Squeeze,* Newsweek, May 19, 1980, at 72; *Working Women: Joys and Sorrows,* U.S. News & World Report, Jan. 15, 1979, at 64.

49. See, *e.g., In re Marriage of Pilatti,* 96 Cal. App. 3d 63, 157 Cal. Rptr. 594 (1979) (holding that ERISA does not preempt California community-property law on retirement benefits and that a spouse's claim of ownership does not constitute assignment, attachment, or alienation).

50. 42 U.S.C. § 402 (Supp. 1982), *amending* 42 U.S.C. § 402 (1974).

51. 9 Pick. 446 (Mass. 1830).

52. Accumulated pension funds total about $650 billion and are growing by 10 percent a year. Private-pension-plan funds account for about three-fifths of that total. *See* Corporate Data Exchange, Inc., Pension Investments: A Social Audit 7 (1979).

The value of the accumulated assets of private pension plans is not remarkably greater than the amount budgeted *annually* for the Department of Health and Human Services. The HHS has a budget larger than that of any *country* in the world except for the Soviet Union and the United States itself. Columbus (Oh.) Citizen-Journal, May 15, 1980, at 2, col. 4.

53. S. Brill, The Teamsters 200–260 (1978).

54. J. Rifkin & R. Barber, The North Will Rise Again 153–169 (1978); Raskin, *Pension Funds Could Be the Unions' Secret Weapon,* Fortune, Dec. 31, 1979, at 64.

55. J. Rifkin & R. Barber, *supra* note 54, at 170–183.

56. *See generally* Chapter 6 *infra,* Investing Pension Funds, at 111.

6 Investing Pension Funds

In August 1980 the AFL-CIO Executive Council approved a committee report establishing the following goals for investment of collectively bargained pension funds:

> To increase employment through reindustrialization including manufacturing, construction, transportation, maritime and other sectors necessary to revitalize the economy. To advance social purposes such as worker housing and health centers. To improve the ability of workers to exercise their rights as shareholders in a coordinated fashion. To exclude from union pension plan investment portfolios companies whose policies are hostile to workers' rights.[1]

This action by the executive council simply made formal positions taken by some labor leaders for some years, namely, that unions should participate in the management of pension funds and that investment of pension funds should promote social objectives. Governments have also taken steps to influence pension-fund-investment decisions. In July 1980 Governor Edmund G. Brown, Jr., of California created The Governor's Public Investment Task Force. In an interim report the task force suggested that "by facilitating the development of new ways to increase the flow of pension capital into productive investment in California—thereby creating more employment opportunities, . . . the State can receive a compensating return in revenues and a decrease in budget expenditures for such costs as welfare and unemployment."[2]

In the 1950s and 1960s when pension plans increased in number and economic importance, unions showed little interest in pension-fund management. When unions insisted on joining or on dominating the management function, their conduct sometimes was notorious rather than exemplary.[3] Professional money managers, principally bankers and insurers, now occupy a commanding position in the investment process. Fund management carries with it a heavy legal responsibility, but it is lucrative. Professional pension-fund managers are unlikely to step aside without resistance or to share readily their function and power. Partici-

---

This chapter was published as R.J. Lynn, *Investing Pension Funds for Social Goals Requires Changing the Law,* 53 U. Colo. L. Rev. 101 (1981). Copyright © 1982 by the University of Colorado Law Review, Inc. Reprinted by permission.

pants in pension plans who are already retired and are drawing benefits might view with understandable skepticism any change in investment practice that could jeopardize the regular flow of retirement income. Moreover, there are serious doubts about the propriety and the wisdom of investing pension funds to promote social goals.

Therefore, the struggle for control of pension funds will be lively and protracted. As the struggle gets underway, what can be said of the legal and political constraints on moving from conventional criteria for the proper investment of pension funds to criteria that include the unconventional? What are the sums at stake? What is the likely outcome?

Legal Constraints

Legal constraints on investment of pension funds consist of federal and state statutes, federal regulations, and court decisions. The particular body of law that applies to a pension plan turns on the origins and the characteristics of the plan: Is the plan created by federal, state, or local government for government employees (a *public* pension plan), or is the plan created by an employer, a union, or an employer and a union together for employees of business and industry (a *private* pension plan)? Is the plan entitled to favorable tax treatment under federal law (a *tax-qualified* plan)? Is the plan a result of collective bargaining (a *negotiated* plan)? Is it a *trusteed* plan?

The law governing the investment of pension funds is a part of the law on fiduciary administration. Formerly, the law on fiduciary administration was heavily case oriented. Now much of it is statutory law. Formerly, the law was primarily state law. Now the law on fiduciary administration includes an important federal element. Whether statutory or nonstatutory, the traditional law on investment of trust funds—funds of decedents' estates, private express (family) trusts, charitable trusts or foundations, and pension trusts (public or private)—stresses maximum earnings consistent with safety of principal. To assist the fiduciary in making decisions, the law on investments usually provides him with the admonitory language of the *prudent-man rule:*

> [The trustee] shall conduct himself faithfully and exercise a sound discretion. He is to observe how men of prudence, discretion and intelligence manage their own affairs, not in regard to speculation, but in regard to the permanent disposition of their funds, considering the probable income, as well as the probable safety of the capital to be invested.[4]

In modified form, the prudent-man rule is a part of ERISA (the

Employee Retirement Income Security Act of 1974),[5] the statute regulating most private pension plans:

> A fiduciary shall discharge his duties . . . solely in the interest of the participants and beneficiaries and . . . with the care, skill, prudence, and diligence under the circumstances then prevailing that a prudent man acting in a like capacity and familiar with such matters would use in the conduct of an enterprise of a like character and with like aims. . . . [6]

The Taft-Hartley act (the Labor Management Relations Act) requires that private pension plans created jointly by an employer and a union be administered "for the sole and exclusive benefit of the employees of such employer and their families and dependents."[7] The Taft-Hartley act antedates ERISA, and ERISA's requirements that a fiduciary act solely in the interest of beneficiaries echoes the words of the earlier statute.

Federal or state statutes, as the case may be, control investment of funded public pension plans. These statutes are usually silent on using other than traditional criteria for investment of funds, although there are occasional exceptions. For example, North Dakota Code § 21-10-05 provides that the state investment board, charged with investing the teachers' retirement fund and the highway patrolmen's retirement fund, invest "in the best interests of the state."[8]

Beneficiaries of pension plans, public or private, are advantaged if the plans are tax-qualified plans, that is, plans so structured and administered that federal-tax deductions, exemptions, exclusions, and deferrals are available. The Internal Revenue Code and treasury regulations on tax qualification indirectly affect investment of pension funds by conditioning tax qualification on conformity to law. For example, Internal Revenue Code § 401(a) requires that a pension plan be administered "for the exclusive benefit of . . . employees or their beneficiaries . . ." to qualify for favorable tax treatment.[9]

Current opinion on the propriety of investing for social purposes takes three forms: (1) Such investing is improper because it violates both the duty of loyalty and the prudent-man rule, or (2) such investing is permissible, or (3) such investing at times is mandatory because interests of participants include nonpecuniary interests. Although the first and the third views are perceptions of the same body of law that are at odds, occasionally they intersect. Either might be viewed uncharitably as originating in a predisposition to find that the law is what one prefers it to be, but that charge, if made at all, is leveled more easily at the third view of mandatory social investing than it is at the first view of social investing as unlawful. The second view, that social investing is permissible, might originate in an effort to accommodate the law to what has occurred without effective challenge during the past fifteen years: investment of university- and college-endowment funds by trustees who use social criteria to govern their decisions as a result of pressure from students, faculty, and concerned persons.

Investing Pension Funds for Social Purposes is Unlawful

The fiduciary's duty of loyalty has been styled "the most fundamental duty" owed by the fiduciary to the beneficiary[10]—the fiduciary is obligated to avoid situations in which his self-interest or the interest of a third person conflicts with the interest of the beneficiary. The duty of loyalty pervades the law on fiduciary administration (administration of decedents' estates, private trusts, charitable trusts, and pension trusts, to name those areas of administration relevant to this inquiry), and it manifests itself in numerous ways. The nature of the duty is easily exemplified by the prohibition of self-dealing. A fiduciary cannot lawfully use trust funds to buy from himself as an individual even though the subject matter of the purchase and the price paid would be the same were the purchase to be made from a stranger.[11] Consequently, when investing, the trustee may not buy securities for the beneficiary's portfolio from himself.

The prudent-man rule of ERISA requires that a fiduciary discharge his duties with respect to a pension plan "solely in the interest of the participants and beneficiaries . . . and for the exclusive purpose of providing benefits to participants and their beneficiaries. . . ."[12] Similar language appears in the Taft-Hartley act,[13] and in the Internal Revenue Code as a requirement for qualifying a pension plan for a favorable tax treatment.[14]

Investing pension funds for social goals does not ordinarily involve self-dealing by the fiduciary, although it might involve a corollary prohibited act, investing to benefit indirectly from the transaction.[15] Investigators find that the breach of the duty of loyalty consists of considering consequences other than furthering the economic interests of participants and beneficiaries when investing pension funds.[16] A pension-fund manager who declines to invest in the stock of a corporation doing business in South Africa may believe that he is hastening the end of apartheid. One who refuses to invest in the stock of a corporation with a history of antiunionization may believe that he is furthering the cause of unionization. However praiseworthy these objectives may be,[17] they do not bear directly on investing to assure benefits to participants and beneficiaries under pension plans.

Investigators also find that investing pension funds for social goals violates the prudent-man rule because it might result in a lower return on investment than is otherwise obtainable.[18] Although the prudent investor might choose an investment bringing a return lower than that otherwise obtainable because the principal is at lower risk, he does not accept the lower return for a nonfinancial purpose. Rather, he seeks the highest return consistent with relative safety of principal. (The fiduciary is not a *guarantor* against loss of principal, but he is obligated to minimize possible loss caused by events beyond his control. When he invests, he hopes for an increase in value, but he considers the possibility of decline in value or complete loss caused by events extraneous to administration of the trust.) Seeking the highest return usually precludes investing for social goals because such investing is less economically advantageous. Furthermore, investigators argue that costless social investing (the social investment being the economic equivalent of a competing investment possibility) might lead to inadequate diversification,[19] an investment requirement under ERISA unless imprudent.[20]

Investigators who have directed their attention principally toward investment of private pension funds under ERISA[21] concede that there might be "some room" under the statute for social investing to promote retirement interests of beneficiaries, but they find that ERISA appears to preclude both investing for social goals to promote interests of nonbeneficiaries and investing for social goals at the cost of "sacrificing financial comparability."[22]

Investing Pension Funds for Social Purposes Is Permissible

Although Scott styles the fiduciary's duty of loyalty the most fundamental duty owed by the fiduciary to the beneficiary,[23] a new section of his treatise *The Law of Trusts* states that trustees acquiring or retaining corporate securities *may* properly consider the "social performance" of the issuing corporation with respect to such matters as environmental pollution, racial discrimination, fair employment, and consumer responsibility. Similarly, trustees holding voting stock *may* properly vote the stock to require "better social behavior" of the issuing corporation. These views are expressed in Section 227.17 of *The Law of Trusts* appropriately titled "Moral considerations as to making and retaining investments."[24] Supporting authority for the new section includes periodical material from the past decade, four state statutes (none of which is a broad-gauge statute on social investing), and an hortatory statement from the trust division of the American Bankers Association. No cases are cited to support Scott's view of social investing.

Although Bogert and Bogert's *The Law of Trusts and Trustees* is undergoing a continuing revision, the new volume on trust investment has no counterpart of Scott's new section on social investing. In a subsection titled "Other Factors to be Considered" (under Section 612 titled "Skill and Prudence Demanded of Trustee in Investing"), there are references to such considerations as inflation and tax consequences, but there is no reference whatever to social criteria for investing.[25]

Permissibility of using social criteria is also advocated by two other investigators[26] who find that benefits lawfully provided to participants and beneficiaries under pension plans are not limited to money payments but can include other benefits such as improved working conditions.[27]

Investing Pension Funds for Social Purposes Is Mandatory

The Conference on Alternative State and Local Policies has reviewed the law on pension investments (federal and state statutes, and case law) and concludes that the law creates a duty "to consider the social, noneconomic impact of pension investment decisions—a principle of social prudence."[28] This duty applies "in particular cases"[29] but has standing equal to that accorded the duty of loyalty.

The conference concedes that no statute or case[30] expressly creates a duty of "social prudence." The conference builds its argument for this duty on the absence of prohibitions on using social criteria for investment and on an insistence that a proper reading of the law on investment makes clear that maximizing return is not a preferred goal, and that, on the contrary, the "common law tradition leans toward the preservation of principal *at minimum risk.*"[31] The conference's reading of investment law is directed toward destroying a so-called myth that social investing is synonymous with illegal political investing that jeopardizes or precludes maximum return on investments.

The Cases

There are two cases commonly cited in connection with investing for social goals. In *Blankenship* v. *Boyle*,[32] trustees of the United Mine Workers of America Welfare and Retirement Fund of 1950, dominated by John L. Lewis of the United Mine Workers of America, allowed excessive fund monies to remain in non-interest-bearing accounts in a bank owned by the United Mine Workers. The trustees invested in stocks of electric-utility companies to induce the utilities to use union-mined coal. Beneficiaries of the fund brought a class-action suit for breach of trust. In giving relief, the court noted that "the Fund has been seriously compromised. . . . It has collaborated with the Union contrary to the trustees' fiduciary duties, and has left excessive sums of money on deposit with the Union's Bank in order to assist the Union."[33] The fund was ordered to cease all relations with the union-owned bank and was prohibited from "operating . . . in a manner designed . . . to afford collateral advantages to the Union or the [coal-mine] operators."[34]

In *Withers* v. *Teachers' Retirement System*,[35] trustees of the Teachers' Retirement System invested in New York City bonds as part of a plan to stave off bankruptcy of the city. Beneficiaries of the system sued for breach of trust. Trustees testified that they feared bankruptcy of the city might result in insolvency of the System because city contributions to the System might cease. In concluding that the plaintiffs had failed to establish a breach of trust, the court noted that

> neither the protection of the jobs of the City's teachers nor the general public welfare were factors which motivated the trustees in their investment decision. The extension of aid to the City was simply a means— the only means, in their assessment—to the legitimate end of preventing the exhaustion of the assets of the [System] in the interest of all of the beneficiaries.[36]

Neither *Blankenship* v. *Boyle* nor *Withers* v. *Teachers' Retirement System* sheds much light on investing for social goals. In *Blankenship*, trustees violated the duty of loyalty. Allowing fund monies to lie in non-interest-bearing accounts in the union-owned bank was clearly detrimental to the interest of the beneficiaries of the fund. In *Withers*, there was no evidence that trustees acted in other than the sole interest of the beneficiaries of the system. The decisions in both cases are consistent with traditional law on fiduciary administration.

Where Are We on Legal Constraints?

What then is the state of the law on investing pension funds for social goals? Although the Conference on Alternative State and Local Policies finds that a duty of social prudence in investing exists in some cases, the conference uncovered no statute or decision expressly creating such duty.[37] One might agree with the conference's contention that the traditional law on investment stresses preservation of principal at minimum risk (rather than stressing maximization of return) without also agreeing that a proper reading of the law or the absence of prohibitions on using social criteria, or a combination of these two factors, supports finding a *duty* to use social criteria in some investment decisions.

Persuasively documented or not, Scott's view that the use of social criteria is permissible makes opposing their use much more difficult than it otherwise would be. For Scott is no mean authority. It is no accident that Section 227 of Scott, *The Law of Trusts,* and the identically numbered section of the Restatement (Second) of *The Law of Trusts* are both titled "Investments Which A Trustee Can Proper ⁄ Make"; Scott was reporter for the preparation of the Restatement (S ond) of *The Law of Trusts*. Few people can prove that they deeply affect the course of the law. Scott probably could have done so. Although Scott falls far short of even implying that social criteria *must* be used, his firm endorsement of permissibility indirectly gives an aura of academic respectability to the arguments of those advocating mandatory use of social criteria. Nonetheless, apart from Scott's new section, there is little support from traditional sources for using social criteria for investment.

There being no express, highly persuasive authority for either mandatory or permissive investing for social goals, does it follow that the views of proponents and opponents are always irreconcilable? Do they ever find themselves on common ground?

Although both camps cite *Withers* v. *Teachers' Retirement System*[38] in support, *Withers* simply is not read in the same way by those holding contrary views regarding the use of nontraditional criteria in investing. Two investigators find that the investment of pension funds in New York City bonds was upheld by the court because the investment aided the city, the principal contributor to the fund, and helped to preserve jobs of beneficiaries.[39] But two other observers find that the investment in *Withers* was made solely in the economic interest of the beneficiaries— the trustees were attempting to assure to beneficiaries the continuing obligation of the city to fund the retirement system.[40] The two camps agree on *consequence,* then, where the unusual facts of a particular case require what would otherwise be an impermissible course of trustee conduct *because that course of conduct is in the economic interest of the beneficiaries.*

Another possibility that is likely to be warmly embraced by the proponents of social investing has been suggested: ratification of such investing by the beneficiaries themselves.[41] Where all beneficiaries of a private express trust are in being, all are *sui juris,* all are fully informed, and all consent, they can ratify or confirm a course of conduct by a trustee that is unlawful.[42] A private trust is a means of making gifts. If donees wish to jeopardize or diminish their gifts, they are free to do so.[43] Transposing this aspect of the law on private express trusts to quasi-public pension trusts is not free from difficulty. Transposition presupposes sufficient similarities in ownership by beneficiaries of private trusts and beneficiaries of pension trusts to justify applying the same law. As we shall see, ownership of pension trusts is a complicated matter.

Political Constraints

Central to union insistence on influencing pension-fund investment decisions is the belief that pension funds are accumulated deferred wages and that workers, both active and retired, own pension funds. This traditional union view was reinforced in 1976 through publication of Peter F. Drucker's *The Unseen Revolution*. Drucker asserted that employees, through pension funds, own enough equity in American business to control business, and that therefore the United States is the first truly socialist country.[44]

That participants in pension plans have a *primary* interest in pension funds cannot be denied. Indeed, their having a primary interest in the financial integrity of the funds is the principal reason for skepticism of using social criteria for investing pension funds: If using social criteria results in a loss of corpus or in a lower return than otherwise would be earned, participants bear the loss or forgo the enhanced return. But it is an oversimplification to assert that sole ownership of pension funds lies in participants in pension plans. The matter of interests in pension funds is complicated.

Identifying interests in pension funds requires inquiry into the creation and the nature of such funds. Private express trusts used by the wealthy to transmit wealth have an identified creator (settlor or testator), beneficiaries of income, and beneficiaries of principal (remaindermen). Creation of the trust is a gratuitous transfer—the creator is a donor, the beneficiaries are donees. Creation of a pension plan is a business transaction, and this is true irrespective of whether the plan is initiated by an employer, by a union, or through collective bargaining. Pension-plan creation is not a gratuitous transfer. Rather, a pension plan is funded principally by the participants themselves, either directly (by a contributory plan) or indirectly (by a noncontributory plan). Although there are income beneficiaries, there are no remaindermen to whom the principal is distributed. Instead, as with a charitable trust, a pension trust might endure forever, accepting periodic contributions and paying benefits to eligible participants.

In the unlikely event that a pension fund originates in employee contributions (payroll deductions) that are unmatched by the employer, the interest of the employee in the fund is clear, but it does not follow that the interest of the employee is the sole interest. Most pension plans are *tax-qualified* pension plans. That is, they are created and administered to take advantage of the federal-income-tax deduction, deferral, exemption, and exclusion devices. Qualified pension plans enjoy an indirect government subsidy through favorable tax treatment, and the commissioner of internal revenue has an interest in such pension plans by virtue of the subsidy.

Most statistically important private pension plans are noncontributory plans. Pension funds originate in employer contributions unmatched by payroll deductions, and the employer contribution is a business expense. Although it might be argued that under these circumstances pension funds are created by consumers who are required to pay a higher price for goods and services than they otherwise would be required to pay, and by stockholders who are required to accept smaller dividends, the employer's contribution commonly is viewed as a deferred wage (so that the contributory plan and the noncontributory plan coalesce). Contributory plans, like noncontributory plans, are usually tax-qualified pension plans. Again, by virtue of the indirect government subsidy the commissioner of internal revenue has an interest in such plans.

Pension plans, whether public or quasi-public (private), are part of the support or income-maintenance system by which those in the work force support those who are not working, and those with higher incomes share with those with lower incomes or no incomes at all. Although the more burdensome consequences of the failure of a private pension plan might fall on the Pension Benefit Guaranty Corporation and the sponsoring employer (through contingent employer liability), some of the fallout from failure will affect all of us. The secretary of labor then has an interest in the financial integrity of many pension funds.[45]

Like social security, public and private pension plans initially were created for the benefit of the covered employee only. But just as social security ultimately brought the family of the employee within the ambit of the social security system, so too public and private pension plans now frequently include the family of the participant as beneficiaries. In both community-property and separate-property (common-law) states, the spouse in particular has a recognized interest in accumulated pension credits on divorce.[46] Although the interests of the family in public and private pensions are not so readily identifiable as are the interests of the family in social security, the interests are at least inchoate and are a factor to be reckoned with when assessing the propriety of investing pension funds.

In sum, participants in plans, families of participants, sponsoring employers and unions, stockholders, government, and the general public—all have an interest in pension funds. Participants unquestionably have a primary interest in such funds, but they do not have a sole interest.

The Sums at Stake

How great are the sums at stake in the fight over control of pension-fund investments? Is the matter of using social criteria for investment of funds of minimal interest because the pension funds that might be affected are of little economic consequence?

Accumulated pension fund assets total about $650 billion.[47] Nearly half are held by federal and state (public) pension systems. The rest are held by private pension plans[48]—those created by employers or unions or by employers and unions together. More often than not, private pension plans are collectively bargained plans. Unions seek a voice in the management of those collectively bargained plans that are now managed by others.

Although it is sometimes suggested that funds are inaccessible in pension plans, accumulated pension funds are in fact invested in the productive capacity of the country through ownership of stocks, bonds, buildings, and land. Pension funds available for investment from time to time originate in periodic contributions to the plan (funding), earnings on investments, and turnover of investments. Amounts available for investment then are at any one time far below the total value of pension fund assets. Even so, the amounts are economically significant. *Institutional investors*—managers of pension funds, university endowments, and the like—strongly affect the course of the stock market.[49] Control of pension fund investments is indeed a matter of economic consequence.

But the consequences of who controls pension-fund investments go beyond the economic. Unionization in the United States has not proceeded apace. In the South and the Southwest, the areas of fastest economic growth, unionization has made little headway. If unions are to survive and grow, they must demonstrate that they effectively represent what they perceive to be the best interests of their members. Some union leaders think that controlling pension-fund-investment decisions will give them the opportunity they need to demonstrate both social concern and economic acumen. Control of pension-fund investments then has a distinctly political overtone.

Conclusion

If participants do not have a sole interest in pension funds but have a primary interest, is a primary interest sufficient justification for insisting as a matter of law that pension funds be invested for the exclusive benefit of participants (and their families) and that social criteria for investing be ignored? A definitive answer to this question is not readily attainable, but a tentative answer is possible.

Conceding that individuals or groups other than the participants have interests in pension funds admits to the possibility that using social criteria for investment will set interest group against interest group, creating dispute and litigation to the profit of lawyers, accountants, and actuaries, and to the loss of participants and their families. Although accumulated pension funds are enormous, sums available for investment on a regular basis are finite. Participants, union leaders, employers, politicians, and government bureaucrats might agree, of course, that a particular investment strategy using social criteria is the ideal path to pursue, but the more likely eventuality is bickering about the criteria to be applied, the mechanics of applying the criteria, and the priority to be accorded competing criteria. Given the contemporary proclivity for litigation, disputes originating in the use of social criteria will land in court, and part of the costs of litigation will be borne by the participants and their families through levies made on pension funds to pay litigation costs. Although participants in pension funds are not the sole equitable owners of such funds, their interest in the funds is unquestionably primary, and a rule of law that investment of funds be pursued for their exclusive benefit is a rational rule that is easily defended on the grounds of tradition, administrative convenience, and economy.

One matter is clear: Given existing statutes (including ERISA), federal regulations, and case law on trust investments, and given the diversity of views on the propriety of investing pension funds for social purposes, fiduciaries will not voluntarily invest substantial sums for social purposes. Historically, fiduciaries have been reluctant to act unless a projected course of conduct is clearly lawful. Where action is of doubtful legality, the tendency has been to let the issue be forced by others. At a minimum the perplexed trustee seeks guidance and approval from a court. After all, the costs of dispute, litigation, and guidance inevitably are borne in part by the trust fund. That being so, there is little incentive for a fiduciary to expose himself to liability when propriety of action is questionable.

Although attempts to accommodate existing law to investing for social goals are not without merit, the game is simply not worth the candle.[50] Barriers raised by statutory words such as "sole and exclusive benefit" are difficult to surmount. If the proponents of social investing are to succeed in requiring that social criteria be used in the investment process, they must seek changes in the law. No other course promises appreciable change in existing fiduciary practice. Where will change in the law first appear?

Pension funds of state and local governments are unusually vulnerable to manipulation for political purposes. Although a public pension fund might originate in part in a healthy contribution from participating employees (so that the primary interest of the participants in the fund is clear), the fund tends to be viewed by politicians as exclusively public and therefore subject to legislative whim. Whatever the law is now on investing pension funds for social purposes, we can reasonably expect strong pressure from a number of sectors—unions, businessmen, and politicians—to give greater flexibility to public-pension-fund trustees who are making investments. Flexibility includes investing to achieve social goals.

If flexibility is introduced at the state and local levels and is not challenged successfully, a change in ERISA (including complementary sections of the Internal Revenue Code) will undoubtedly be sought. In that event, we can expect a lively discussion of the nature and purpose of pension funds. The discussion is important. Proper disposition of pension funds affects us all.

Notes

1. AFL-CIO, Investment of Union Pension Funds iii (1980).

2. Interim Report, [California] Governor's Public Investment Task Force 2 (Mar. 1981). A final report by the task force was issued in October 1981.

3. Cook, *The most abused, misused pension fund in America,* Forbes, Nov. 10, 1980, at 69; *Union Corruption Worse Than Ever,* U.S. News & World Report, Sept. 8, 1980, at 33.

4. *Harvard College v. Amory,* 9 Pick. 446, 461 (Mass. 1830).

5. For a summary of the salient features of ERISA, see Chapter 5 *supra,* The Employee Retirement Income Security Act (ERISA), at 85.

6. Employee Retirement Income Security Act of 1974 § 404(a)(1)(B); 29 U.S.C. § 1104(a)(1)(B) (1976).

7. Labor Management Relations (Taft-Hartley) Act of 1947 § 302(c)(5), 29 U.S.C. § 186(c)(5) (1976).

8. N.D. Cent. Code § 21–10–05 (1978).

9. I.R.C. § 401(a), 26 U.S.C. § 401(a) (1976).

10. 2 A. Scott, The Law of Trusts § 170 (3d ed. 1967).

11. *Id.* § 170.12.

12. Employee Retirement Income Security Act of 1974 § 404(a)(1)(A), 29 U.S.C. § 1104(a)(1)(A) (1976).

13. Labor Management Relations (Taft-Hartley) Act of 1947 § 302(c)(5), 29 U.S.C. § 186(c)(5) (1976).

14. I.R.C. § 401(a), 26 U.S.C. § 401(a) (1976).

15. In *Blankenship v. Boyle,* 329 F.Supp. 1089 (D.D.C. 1971), trustees of a union-dominated miners' pension fund invested in stocks of electric utilities to induce the utilities to buy union-mined coal, thus benefiting the union indirectly.

16. Langbein & Posner, *Social Investing and the Law of Trusts,* 79 Mich. L. Rev. 72, 96 (1980).

17. In addition to promoting unionization, creating worker housing, and maintaining jobs, social purposes include equal employment opportunity, environmental protection, consumer protection, encouraging small businesses, and ending racism. Social goals getting current attention are job creation and maintenance. It has been charged that existing institutional and legal constraints on pension-fund investment create a bias against investment in the northeast-midwest regions of the United States, and against small, new, and expanding firms. P. Tropper & A. Kaufman, Pension Power for Economic Development i (Northeast-Midwest Institute Dec. 1980).

18. Langbein & Posner, *Social Investing and the Law of Trusts,* 79 Mich L. Rev. 72, 98 (1980).

19. *Id.* 85–92, 98–99.

20. Employee Retirement Income Security Act of 1974 § 404(a)(1)(C), 29 U.S.C. § 1104(a)(1)(C) (1976).

21. Hutchinson & Cole, *Legal Standards Governing Investment of Pension Assets for Social and Political Goals,* 128 U. Pa. L. Rev. 1340 (1980).

22. *Id.* 1388.

23. 2 A. Scott, The Law of Trusts § 170 (3d ed. 1967).

24. 3 *Id.* § 227.17 (Supp. 1981).

25. G.G. Bogert & G.T. Bogert, The Law of Trusts and Trustees § 612 (1980).

26. Ravikoff & Curzan, *Social Responsibility in Investment Policy and the Prudent Man Rule,* 68 Calif. L. Rev. 518 (1980).

27. *Id.* 523.

28. M. Leibig, Social Investments and the Law 8 (Aug. 1980).

29. *Id.* 32.

30. *Id.*

31. *Id.* 7.

32. 329 F.Supp. 1089 (D.D.C. 1971), *aff'd mem.*, 511 F.2d 447 (D.C. Cir. 1975).

33. *Id.* 1112.

34. *Id.* 1113.

35. 447 F.Supp. 1248 (S.D.N.Y. 1978), *aff'd mem.*, 595 F.2d 1210 (2d Cir. 1979).

36. 447 F.Supp. at 1256.

37. M. Leibig, Social Investments and the Law 63 (Aug. 1980).

38. 447 F.Supp. 1248 (S.D.N.Y. 1978), *aff'd mem.*, 595 F.2d 1210 (2d Cir. 1979).

39. Ravikoff & Curzan, *Social Responsibility in Investment Policy and the Prudent Man Rule,* 68 Calif. L. Rev. 518, 523 (1980).

40. Langbein & Posner, *Social Investing and the Law of Trusts,* 79 Mich. L. Rev. 72, 101–102 (1980).

41. *Id.* 105–107.

42. 3 A. Scott, The Law of Trusts § 218 (3d ed. 1967).

43. This is so in the absence of a spendthrift clause. 2 A. Scott, The Law of Trusts § 151 (3d ed. 1967). ERISA has a spendthrift provision. Employee Retirement Income Security Act of 1974 § 206(d), 29 U.S.C. § 1056(d) (1976).

44. P. Drucker, The Unseen Revolution 1 (1976).

45. Ian D. Lanoff, Administrator, Office of Pension and Welfare Benefit Programs, U.S. Department of Labor, states that investing for social goals that is costless economically is permissible under ERISA. Lanoff, *The Social Investment of Private Pension Plan Assets: May It Be Done Lawfully under ERISA?,* 31 Lab. L. J. 387, 392 (1980).

46. *See, e.g., In re Marriage of Pilatti,* 96 Cal. App. 3d 63, 157 Cal. Rptr. 594 (1979), *cert. den.* 445 U.S. 916 (1980).

47. Final Report [California] Governor's Public Investment Task Force ix (Oct. 1981).

48. U.S. Dep't of Labor, Labor-Management Services Adm., Pension and Welfare Benefit Programs, The Prudence Rule and Pension Plan Investments Under ERISA 7 (1980).

49. Newsweek, March 22, 1971, at 94.

50. *See, e.g.,* Schotland's list of conditions essential to selecting or avoiding investments using nonfinancial criteria. Schotland, *Should Pension Funds Be Used to Achieve ''Social'' Goals?,* Trusts & Estates, Nov. 1980, at 26, 33–34. Earlier articles in this three part series are found in Trusts & Estates, Sept. 1980, at 10, and Trusts & Estates, Oct. 1980, at 27.

7 Reducing Pension Costs

Providing support payments to numerous beneficiaries of the support or income-maintenance system has become burdensome on a year-to-year basis, but the matter of immediate burden aside, there is reason to think that the pension components of the system, whether public, like OASDI (Old Age, Survivors, and Disability Insurance under social security), or quasi-public, like private pensions, will be in severe financial difficulties in the years ahead. Some of those financial difficulties originate in population changes, others in insufficient funding. But whatever the cause of the difficulty, there is general agreement that it is essential to determine as quickly as possible how to control pension costs.

The income-maintenance system is chaotic. Programs overlap, and there is inefficiency and waste in providing benefits. Not surprisingly, the pension components of the income-maintenance system provide disability and retirement benefits inefficiently. Because the pension system is complex, reducing pension costs through reducing duplication and waste will not be easy. Nonetheless, three measures to reduce pension costs can be adopted without great delay: (1) The normal retirement age can be raised and incentives to retire early can be reduced. (2) An equitable system of offsets can be adopted to ensure that disability or retirement income, irrespective of pension source, is *replacement* of preretirement, earned income and does not exceed preretirement, earned income. (3) Pensions can be indexed sparingly, and an index can be used that is appropriate to the task of assuring to the disabled and the retired adequate income that does not exceed preretirement, earned income.

Full Employment

The most effective way to reduce the costs of support payments—including pensions—is to change the conditions that create the call for such payments. To the extent that we can both insist on and achieve full employment, we can reduce the costs of providing welfare, unemploy-

---

This chapter is drawn from R.J. Lynn, *Reducing Pension Costs Now: Three Suggestions*, 23 Ariz. L. Rev. 689 (1981). Copyright © by the Arizona Board of Regents. Reprinted by permission.

ment compensation, disability pensions, and old-age pensions. Full employment in this context means just that—getting into the work force and keeping in the work force as many people as feasible regardless of age, disability, race, religion, national origin, sex, or sexual preference.

Although feasible, full employment accommodates the desire for early retirement where the burden of providing this option does not fall too heavily on those in the work force; concurrently, it emphasizes remaining in the work force in some capacity throughout life. Feasible full employment takes account of mothers or fathers who prefer to remain with infants and small children rather than entrust them to relatives or daycare centers, but it recognizes the fact that women, including women with young children, are a permanent part of the work force and are entitled to equality with men.[1] Feasible full employment requires rethinking well-meant but sometimes pernicious efforts to raise the minimum wage. Both teenagers and society might be better off if adolescents and some other groups in the population such as the severely handicapped were at work at a wage that is substantially lower than that paid to other segments of the work force. One need not invoke the work ethic to demonstrate that even work at a comparatively low wage is preferable to long periods of empty idleness.

Lack of job opportunities open to those seeking work, long layoffs of those regularly employed, and excessive amounts of so-called make-work of various kinds[2] contribute heavily to the costs of support borne by those who are working. Therefore, feasible full employment requires determining how to maintain a stable economy, how to maintain the economic growth that provides jobs,[3] and how to slow the growth of government and service employment where it has become clear that such growth is unhealthy. Full employment requires facing up to the fact that much work is, and will continue to be, distasteful to some extent and that not all who wish to do so can engage in work that they find meaningful. Even with the explosive growth of professional sports, not all who have prepared for and who aspire to professional sports careers can be accommodated. The number of professional historians who can practice their craft on a full-time basis is limited. A pattern of preparation for and aspiration to a particular career choice, followed by disappointed expectations, repeats itself with regrettable frequency in numerous contexts.

There are, and will continue to be, groups within the population who are not in the work force and remain outside it for either an appreciable period of time or as long as life lasts. Among those outside the work force for an appreciable period of time are children and young adults in school on a full-time basis and mothers or fathers of small children who remain with their children rather than enter the work force. Some of the mentally or physically disabled are absent from the work force for long periods, and some of the severely disabled are absent for their lifetimes. The very old (those in their late seventies and beyond) traditionally do not work, and even an enlightened work force is unlikely to encourage the very old to continue working. It is one thing to discourage early retirement (thus keeping those in their fifties and sixties engaged in work), and it is another to insist on work by those whose productivity might prove to be marginal at best because of advanced age and impaired agility. In sum, although we might reasonably expect to reduce the costs of support payments to some extent by insisting on and achieving full employment, there are some groups within the population who understandably do not work in the conventional sense, and who are not expected to do so because of age, or engagement in other tasks, or disability.

There are even some people who might work but do not so choose. Within this group are both those of inherited wealth who do not work and those receiving support payments who refuse to work (despite the existence of devices within the support system intended to induce work). Conventionally, we do not think of the nonworking wealthy as being supported by the work force, although of course some are. With the exception of the share of a deceased spouse's wealth taken by or awarded to the surviving spouse of a marriage of long duration, inherited wealth is *unearned income*. Just as a pension is realistically a claim to such goods and services provided by the work force as are available for distribution from time to time, so too wealth, whether accumulated or inherited, is a claim to resources, and at any particular time, essential resources are always limited and are being allocated to competing claimants. In an ideal world, there might be no so-called idle rich, on the one hand, or welfare frauds,[4] on the other, but we have not achieved an ideal world, and we are not likely to do so. Considerable time and effort have gone into investigating and reporting on both the idle rich and welfare frauds, with no visible change in the attitudes of either. Although feasible full employment seeks to keep in the work force as many people as can reasonably be accommodated, the costs required to bring in the recalcitrant at times unquestionably will exceed the benefits achieved, and therefore pursuit of the recalcitrant should be undertaken with skepticism.

Keeping the Work Force at Work

Both public pensions (like those payable under social security) and quasi-public pensions (originating in numerous plans created by business, labor, or the two in concert) are part of the income-transfer (or transfer-payments) system by which those who are working share with those who are not, and those with higher incomes share with those of lower incomes or no incomes at all. Some income transfers occur without the mediation of government, but by far the most important income transfers occur under federal law and are bottomed on the federal income tax. In the federal departments engaged in income transfers, the Department of Health and Human Services dispenses the most money, principally in social security benefits. Beneficiaries of social security payments include the retired and the disabled.

Because the average life span can be predicted with considerable certainty, the number of people receiving social security retirement benefits from year to year can be predicted with considerable certainty. As the number of elderly increases, the costs of providing retirement benefits increase, based on such increased numbers alone. But there being larger numbers of recipients from year to year does not in itself account for the mounting costs of providing retirement benefits. Social security payments are *indexed,* that is, they are tied to a variable, and they rise as prices rise. And from time to time additional occupations or groups have been *blanketed in* (that is, given coverage under social security), creating benefit costs not necessarily altogether borne by the groups added.

Disability pensions became available under social security in 1956. Whether a person is chronologically old is a matter of elapsed time; whether a person is disabled is a matter of opinion. Between 1965 and 1978 the number of people receiving disability pensions under social security tripled.[5]

Retirement—to say nothing of early retirement—is a comparatively new notion. Formerly, when numerous occupations were hazardous (so that accidental death was more frequent than it is now) and deadly diseases were common, the average life span was shorter. Withdrawing from the work force because of age was the exception; people died while still employed. But as the proportion of "killing" jobs declined, and control of many insidious diseases was achieved, the average life span lengthened. Prosperity and relative abundance both permitted and encouraged the creation of a new leisure class consisting of retired employees and their spouses.[6] Just fifty years ago the number of retired in the population was small. Today the number of retired is in the millions, supported by those who work.

It is actual retirement of a member of the work force that puts a burden on those remaining in the work force and those thereafter entering the work force. For a withdrawal from work usually draws in its wake support or income-maintenance payments, most commonly pensions. Nonetheless, both the time at which a person *might* retire (irrespective of whether he in fact does so) and the time at which a person *must* retire (although in fact he retires at an earlier time) are of interest to those in the work force because the possibility of early retirement and the specter of *mandatory* (forced) retirement affect actual retirement.

The normal retirement age for social security purposes is sixty-five, just as it is for numerous other public and private pension plans. Social security permits early retirement at age sixty-two.[7] Some public and private pension plans permit early retirement at an age younger than sixty-two, and some permit retirement after a specified number of years of service, irrespective of age, thus inviting early retirement. Mandatory retirement at age seventy is still lawful in most lines of work.[8] In sum, existing pension systems invite those in the work force to retire when in their sixties, if not before, and require retirement of those entering their seventies.

Pension costs can be reduced by raising the normal retirement age (when a full pension becomes payable), and by deemphasizing early retirement (when a pension often sufficient to induce retirement is payable). We can reduce pension costs, release funds for investment, and add to the gross national product simply by keeping the work force at work.

Raising the Normal Retirement Age

It has been suggested that raising the normal retirement age under social security from sixty-five to, say, seventy must be deferred until the end of this century because raising the age before that time breaks the so-called social contract that sustains the system.[9] The notion is that a change of this particular kind can never be made because such a change would be unfair to those expecting to retire at sixty-five.

There are several observations that should be made with respect to the social contract. First, and perhaps most significantly, the burden of this compact is borne in part by people who were either unborn when the compact was made or who had little significant voice in setting its terms. Although people in their sixties, seventies, and eighties who are drawing social security benefits were alive when the social security system was adopted, people in their twenties and thirties who must bear part of the costs were not. It is one thing to be born advantaged by a social contract that puts a high premium on freedom of speech. It is quite another to be born deprived in advance of a significant part of earned income to provide for one's predecessors.

Second, if there is a social contract, might there not be an inquiry into what the original contract encompassed? At its inception, social security was intended to provide a retirement income *base;* it was not intended to provide *replacement income,* as that term is now generally understood. Replacement income was visualized (somewhat unrealistically) as originating in part in private savings and investments, and in private pension plans. Nonetheless, for many aged people, social security income has been, and still is, virtually the sole source of retirement income. That being so, there has been and will continue to be effective political pressure brought to bear to make social security retirement income an earned-income replacement. Furthermore, medicare, which for many retired people is just as important as the social security retirement component, was added to social security three decades after its inception, and medicare has added enormous costs to the public support system.

Third, if we assume both a social contract and the general desirability of fulfilling that contract, we must then consider the weight of the burden that the work force can reasonably be expected to bear, and having done so, we must take account of what in all probability will occur. The inevitable conclusion is that the work force can be reasonably expected to forgo some consumption to provide for those in the population who cannot reasonably be expected to support themselves. But to think that the work force will support in relative comfort comparatively large numbers of people capable of supporting themselves is to dream. Human nature being what it is, the social contract in its present wasteful form will be broken.

Is it feasible to keep the elderly at work? Will keeping them at work frustrate the young seeking entry into the work force and promotion after employment? Will keeping the elderly at work merely exacerbate the problem of unemployment?

Within every age group there are variations in health. People between the ages of fifty and seventy-five are less likely to be healthy than people between the ages of twenty and forty-five, but even so, there are many over fifty in good health, capable of working and willing to work. Although those in their seventies are less likely to be in good health than those in their fifties, there are many people in their seventies in good health, capable of working and willing to work. Some possess extraordinary skills. Not all are wise, but some have the wisdom that is acquired from long experience. It is in the best interests of neither the work force nor the individual forced from work to allow such skills and wisdom to lie unused.

Whether members of the work force should be encouraged to retire early, on the one hand, or forced to retire (irrespective of age), on the other, ought to be decided on the basis of a number of factors of which age is only one.[10] For example, in some lines of work, although the number of positions available fluctuates from time to time, the number is always limited. Because the number of positions to be filled from year to year cannot be predicted with certainty, entry into and exit from the occupational group cannot be regulated so as to assure work to all of those who are prepared to take it in a given year. In that event it might be in the public interest both to *require* retirement of those who have already experienced a long and fulfilling career and to *encourage* early retirement of sufficient numbers of others in the occupational group to make way for the new entrants. Adjustments of this kind are not easy to make, but it is arguably better to think through the possibility of such adjustments in advance and to try to set fair standards for entry into and exit from an occupational group rather than have such adjustments made on an ad hoc basis, with its concomitant aspect of arbitrariness and resulting ill-will.

Another factor that should be considered in fixing retirement principles is the feasibility of the retiree's continuing to work on a part-time basis or undertaking a second (or third) career, on either a full-time or a part-time basis. Although vigor declines with age, the decline is usually gradual, not precipitous. There is nothing about either the human body, despite the physiology of aging, or the nature of work in America that makes retirement an all-or-nothing proposition. Just as it is in the public interest that the young and the severely handicapped be employed at a wage somewhat lower than that earned by more mature or able-bodied employees, so too it is in the public interest to structure public and private pension plans in such a way that people who can work continue to do so, even if the work is part-time or the wage lower than that theretofore earned.

One of the ways in which the elderly can continue to work full time or part time beyond a so-called normal retirement age is to spend a substantial amount of the workday teaching the young or the inexperienced. In nearly all lines of work, various skills are acquired on the job and nowhere else. Experienced employees can help the inexperienced acquire needed skills more quickly. Thus older employees to whom teaching is congenial can remain productive themselves and can improve productivity generally by remaining on the job in a teaching capacity. Similarly, many who have taught throughout life prefer to teach as long as they are permitted to do so. As vigor declines, they might be encouraged to retire but to continue to teach part-time, with adjustments in pension payments made to reflect the principle that postretirement income not exceed preretirement income. Once we view the entire support or income-maintenance system, including pensions, as principally directed toward affording *replacement* income, we can adjust pension payments in individual cases in accordance with that objective.

Some occupations are so taxing physically or mentally (or both) that they do not lend themselves to pursuit throughout a working lifetime on a full-time basis and they afford limited teaching possibilities. For example, even with advanced technology and improved mechanical equipment, much construction work is exceptionally demanding, giving the edge to younger, stronger, and more vigorous employees. In such lines of work, keeping people in the work force requires periodic shifting of employees to less strenuous tasks within an occupation, if feasible, or assisting them to shift to less strenuous work in some other vocation. In this connection, a national *job-opportunity network* can be developed. In what is touted as the computer age, it is a scandal that people seeking work and employers seeking employees so frequently are brought together in an unsystematic and inefficient way.[11]

Changing jobs requires a willingness by employers to accept qualified applicants for work, irrespective of age, and changing jobs often requires job retraining. American experience in both matters leaves much to be desired. Despite legal prohibitions against discrimination in employment based on age, such discrimination persists, in part because unlawful discrimination is difficult to prove. Job retraining for the elderly and their reentry into the work force traditionally have been regarded as difficulties to be overcome by individuals rather than as economic or social problems. To the extent that achieving feasible full employment depends on job retraining and reentry into the work force, progress is likely to be slow.

Keeping people at work in a preferred career choice as long as possible, irrespective of age, shifting some in the work force from demanding work to less demanding tasks as middle age sets in, adapting the work place to part-time employment, and retraining where required, all presuppose substantially good health of those encouraged to remain at work. Although Americans support the most expensive health-care system in the world, they are not as healthy as they might be.[12] Poor health is said to force eight times as many men from employment as does mandatory retirement.[13] To some extent poor health is a consequence of the use of alcohol, tobacco, and drugs. Poor health is sometimes attributable to chance (including genetic chance). If we are to keep people at work as long as possible, a higher degree of success in coping with the infirmities associated with aging is essential. As a matter of immediate administrative convenience (and as an accommodation to those who wish to cease work), it is sometimes easier to certify an ailing person as disabled than it is to puzzle out the cause of an infirmity. The dramatic increase in the number of those receiving disability pensions under social security attests to the generosity built into the definition of *disability* and to the discretion given to those assessing state of health.

A healthy population is crucial to getting people into the work force and keeping them there as long as possible. During the past half-century medicine has made great strides, but health care in the United States understandably is still directed largely to treatment of disease and to sustaining the disabled, not rehabilitating them.[14] Physician training stresses treatment, and health facilities are most often places for treatment. To a considerable extent, this state of affairs is inevitable—we cannot sensibly assume that if we tripled the number of gymnasiums and running tracks, we would have a responsive reduction in the number of hospitals. Improving the health of Americans over the life span will take time, and we cannot postulate success in improving health to such an extent that substantially all in the work force will remain capable of working until death. The evidence runs to the contrary.

Deemphasizing Early Retirement

People who need not be drawing income-maintenance benefits such as welfare, unemployment benefits, disability pensions, or retirement pensions, add unnecessarily to the burden of income-maintenance costs. To the extent that people of working age can be integrated into the work force and kept there during their working lives, we can reduce income-maintenance costs. In recent years, however, the minimum wage (which tends to curtail entry into the work force) has steadily risen, and early retirement (which tends to remove an employee from work well before the end of his working life) has been encouraged under both public and private pension plans. Mandatory retirement forces many from the work force who are unquestionably capable of work. And disability looms as never before as a drain on income-maintenance funds. Pension costs are enhanced by the tendency to retire early, by forcing productive employees out of the work force solely on the basis of age, and by granting disability pensions indiscriminately. Early retirement, mandatory retirement, and disability adjudication and compensation need reexamination. Costs are out of hand now, and we cannot wait until the year 2000 to bring them under control.

If we are serious about reducing pension costs, we must abandon early retirement as a preference, cease to encourage it, and regard it as exceptional. We can change attitudes toward early retirement in a number of ways.

One way to make early retirement less attractive is to make work more tolerable. Much work is and will continue to be hard, demanding, and distasteful. It does not follow that we cannot improve working conditions. Our rush to get work done need not always preclude considering how it is done. Although democratizing the work place is suggested from time to time as a means of making work more attractive,[15] working conditions can be improved by methods short of proliferating committees. For example, *flex-time* (varying the time of arrival at and departure from work) can be remarkably helpful to the employee who is the parent (frequently the single parent) of infants or children of school age. We can vary the length of the workday and workweek. The half-time employee is seldom accorded the same status as the full-time employee, regardless of his relative productivity. In sum, just as age sixty-five is not immutable as the age of normal retirement, so too the eight-to-five day, the eight-hour day, and the five-day workweek are not immutable for purposes of work.

Similarly, we can make early retirement less attractive by trying to provide alternative lines of work to those who have worked long under trying conditions and want to quit. We conventionally think of manual laborers as particularly afflicted by poor working conditions, but numerous lines of work are difficult and enervating. If employees long at work under trying circumstances can be directed to more attractive work rather than to subsidized idleness, both they and the rest of the work force are better off. (Instead of promising the novice fireman a pension after twenty years of service, why not offer him training for alternative employment?)

Probably the most effective way to discourage early retirement is to make it less attractive economically. If benefits payable on early retirement substantially approximate benefits payable at normal retirement age, those in the work force marginally motivated to work choose early retirement. The situation here is almost identical to that encountered when unemployment benefits approximate earned income—there is little incentive to work.[16] If we wish to reduce pension costs, we must face up to the price paid by having transformed early retirement into normal retirement.

Undesirable Side-Effects?

If early retirement were not encouraged and mandatory retirement were severely restricted, it is possible that some in the work force who would otherwise have retired will remain in the work force simply to draw their pay, continuing as unproductive employees. Mandatory retirement frequently is defended on the ground that it impersonally requires withdrawal from the work force of some who are no longer efficient.

If legal devices that remove older employees from the work force are modified to encourage them to continue working as long as feasible, it is indeed true that a consequence might be that inefficient employees will remain on the job in significant numbers. Because mandatory retirement has been the norm for a long time in many occupations, we have some knowledge of the effects of compulsory withdrawal from the work force. Raising the age of mandatory retirement and eliminating it altogether with respect to some lines of work are recent phenomena. Therefore we cannot predict with assurance what results will follow. Nonetheless, this can be said: There are in all lines of work employees who are inefficient, irrespective of age. Aging can, and no doubt does, affect productivity, but is only one of a number of factors. At some time, of course, age becomes the sole factor. Although it might be that encouraging older employees to remain on the job will result in significant numbers of older employees who are unproductive in the work force, we do not know that such a consequence would ensue; if it were to occur, it would not be a unique state of affairs. Like many other labor problems, it would have to be dealt with on a case-by-case basis.

Neither the unemployed nor the retired are in the work force, and both groups are supported by the work force. The fewer the number of people in each group, the lighter the burden on the work force. If the aging and the elderly remain at work, the number of unemployed might temporarily rise because job openings attributable to retirement will be deferred for a time. In that event, the work force will not be advantaged because reduced pension costs will be offset by increased unemployment costs.

This consequence is possible, perhaps even probable. But it is not inevitable. First, measures to keep the work force at work can be phased in gradually. Second, an undesirably high rate of unemployment has been with us for some time.[17] Government attempts at job training and job creation have had mixed results.[18] We are about to turn to the private sector to increase capital expenditures, reduce unemployment, and improve productivity. If this effort proves to be successful, keeping the aging at work will result in a net gain. If it does not, we shall be none the worse for having given the matter a try.

Coordinating Benefits (Offsetting)

Double-dipping—drawing disability or retirement benefits from more than one source,[19] often tax-supported sources—is usually explicitly or implicitly characterized as antisocial. Pensioners not so fortunate as to draw from more than one source regard the practice as unfair. Taxpayers think that the practice borders on fraud.

Whether double-dipping is inequitable turns on our perceptions of the principal objectives of the support or income-maintenance system in the United States, including disability and retirement pensions. One objective of the income-maintenance system supported by the work force is to provide the unemployed, the injured, the disabled, or the retired employee with *replacement* income—that is, an income that approximates preretirement, earned income but that does not exceed preretirement, earned income as adjusted for inflation.[20] A familiar axiom of insurance law is that a contract of insurance (other than life) is a contract of indemnity. The insured is to be compensated for loss but not *over*compensated. The income-maintenance system is a system of social insurance. A participant in the system is entitled to replacement income but no more than that.

It follows that in some cases double-dipping is not inequitable because the total amount of income received from multiple income-maintenance sources does not exceed preretirement, earned income. Indeed, in some instances, income received by a disabled or retired employee would fall short of adequate income in the absence of double-dipping. For example, it is not remarkable for a married woman to have worked part-time during her twenties and thirties at employment where she was covered by social security. At age forty-five she finds herself widowed and not eligible for social security benefits based on either her own work record or that of her deceased spouse. Forced into the work force on a full-time basis at a time when she is likely to be discriminated against because of age, to say nothing of sex,[21] she takes employment at a relatively low wage with a municipality offering a pension plan that pays modest retirement benefits. If she leaves the work force either voluntarily or involuntarily in her sixties, and draws both her municipal pension and social security benefits based either on her own work record or that of her deceased spouse, it is unlikely that her total income will exceed preretirement, earned income. Where total income from multiple pension sources does not exceed preretirement, earned income, as in this kind of case, double-dipping cannot rationally be viewed as inequitable.

Some General Consideration

Double-dipping that results in disability or retirement income exceeding preretirement earned income invites setting a ceiling on disability or retirement benefits and creating controls to assure that the ceiling is not exceeded. Generally speaking, there has been no clear articulation of a ceiling on disability or retirement income, and existing controls have taken the form of *offsets*—a dollar-for-dollar reduction in one kind of tax-supported benefit to the extent that a similar benefit originates in a comparable tax-supported source. Denying or reducing income-maintenance benefits because the applicant for, or beneficiary of, such benefits has other sources of income is an old and pervasive device for controlling costs. A familiar example of the device is the much deplored *means test* for determining eligibility for welfare benefits. From time to time abolition of the means test is urged because inquiry into the financial resources of an applicant is deemed to be degrading. Whatever it is called, the means test is unlikely to disappear. If those seeking public office are required to make full disclosure of means as a condition of public employment paid for by taxpayers,[22] *a fortiori* full disclosure of means by those seeking disability or retirement income provided by the work force can be required. It is not disclosure that is demeaning; it is the scope and the method of disclosure that bring disclosure into disrepute. From the fact that disclosure of income sources causes difficulties it does not follow that it can be abandoned.

A ceiling on disability or retirement income should originate in what a beneficiary's earned income was and an assessment of what the work force can afford to provide willingly to nonworking segments of the population. Using preretirement earned income as a ceiling on disability or retirement income implicitly assumes that preretirement earned income is sufficient to provide an adequate standard of living. Clearly, that is not always the case. When preretirement earned income does not provide an adequate standard of living, it is pointless to consider using preretirement earned income as a ceiling on disability or retirement income because the pensioner probably was a beneficiary of the income-maintenance system while in the work force. In short, we are not dealing with the troublesome kinds of cases where benefit formulas or double-dipping or indexing produces disproportionate disability or retirement incomes that provoke resentment among those still working.

Similarly, when determining whether disability or retirement income can equal rather than exceed preretirement earned income, we should recognize the desirability of differentiating kinds of cases to the extent that differentiation is administratively feasible. For example, a disabled husband and father in his midthirties might be sensibly viewed as having income-maintenance requirements that are different from those of the retired couple in their seventies.

In sum, because disability or retirement income is replacement income, it should not ordinarily exceed preretirement earned income, and coordination of benefits should be used to assure that it does not. However, if preretirement earned income fails to provide an adequate standard of living, it is an inappropriate ceiling on disability or retirement income. And if income-maintenance requirements are significantly different after disability or retirement than they are before disability or retirement, preretirement earned income is a relevant factor in fixing the support payment, but it should not be decisive.

Setting a ceiling on disability or retirement income and refining controls for assuring that the ceiling is not exceeded will assist in controlling pension costs. Eliminating inequitable double-dipping will not reduce pension costs in the dramatic way that achieving feasible full employment will reduce costs, but the savings will be nonetheless significant, and public perceptions of the income-maintenance system will be improved.

Multiple Sources

It is not always an easy task to determine which pension systems or plans fall within those multiple-income maintenance sources that are, or might become, subject to controls for achieving equitable replacement income. Candidates mentioned with some frequency include federal civil-service pensions, military pensions, veterans pensions, state and municipal civil-service pensions, and social security. All have the common characteristic of being sponsored by government. Private pensions are not sponsored by government directly, but their creation is attributable in part to federal-income-tax deduction, exclusion, deferral, and exemption devices, and nearly all are subject to federal regulation. Proliferation of private pensions is attributable in part to a U.S. Court of Appeals decision.[23] Often, accumulated private pension funds ostensibly are created solely by employers, but the actual costs of creating such funds are borne by employees, stockholders, and purchasers of goods. When private pension plans falling under ERISA fail, the costs of failure are borne by successful plans through the medium of the Pension Benefit Guaranty Corporation. Private pensions then are a part of the income-transfer system by which those who are working share with those who are not, and those receiving higher incomes share with those of lower incomes or no incomes at all. They are at least quasi-public in nature, and although they can be and are differentiated from public pensions, private pensions and public pensions have more common than divergent characteristics. Resistance to including private pensions within the array of multiple-income maintenance sources subject to controls is undoubtedly great, but they cannot rationally be excluded, and it is unlikely that a work force perceiving itself as unduly burdened by pension costs will permit exclusion.

Creating Offsets

Coordination of benefits and offsets (or *setoffs*) are well-established techniques for controlling pension costs. As pressures for reducing costs intensify, they will be used more frequently. The task ahead is to use them fairly. How should we go about constructing offsets that work fairly?

Where a beneficiary of the income-maintenance system is entitled to benefits from more than one source, the inclination of each source is to reduce its own payment to the extent that benefits are payable from another source or sources. For example, if A is entitled to retirement benefits from both public source X and public source Y, public source X might reduce its benefits payable to A to the extent that A is entitled to benefits payable by public source Y. As indicated earlier, such reduction of benefits will deprive A of adequate income if total income from sources X and Y, absent offsetting, will not exceed preretirement, earned income. Furthermore, if both source X and Y insist on offsetting to the extent that A is entitled to benefits from the other source, offsetting more than reduces benefits—it altogether eliminates them.

If preretirement earned income was sufficient to provide an adequate standard of living (so that preretirement earned income can be used as a ceiling on disability or retirement income), and if A is entitled to disability or retirement benefits from multiple sources that cumulatively exceed preretirement earned income (so that offsetting is appropriate), the multiple sources of benefits might provide replacement income in proportion to the present values of the benefits payable from each source when benefit payments from multiple sources begin. For example, if A draws a military (unfunded) pension, retires from a second career and is entitled to a municipal (unfunded) pension, the respective sources of A's two unfunded pensions will bear the expense of A's total benefits (not exceeding replacement income) in proportion to the present values of the benefits payable from each source when A retires for the second time.

Circumstances calling for the use of offsets are frequently much more complicated than those of the forgoing example. Therefore, creating a system of offsets that works fairly and is administratively feasible will be difficult and time-consuming. The nature of offsetting inevitably encourages dispute and litigation. The history of the income-maintenance system precludes the ready creation of offsetting formulas. Although most of the elements of the income-maintenance system are new, some are old. The retirement and disability pension system is part public and part quasi-public (private). Some pension funds originate solely in employer contributions, and others originate in part in employee contributions. Some pension plans are unfunded. Some pension plans pay a fixed annuity to a beneficiary, and others pay a variable annuity. Private pension plans frequently require offsetting by *integration* of plan benefits with social security benefits,[24] but the offsetting that is anticipated by a pension plan does not exhaust all possibilities for offsetting.

Furthermore, perceptions of the elements in the income-maintenance system vary from group to group, and change over time. There are those receiving benefits from the system and there are those still in the work force. There is a large group of people engaged in servicing the system: bankers, insurers, investment counselors, lawyers, accountants, actuaries, social workers, computer experts, investigators, and a great army of clerks. Those receiving benefits perceive them not as gratuities but as an entitlement received as a matter of right. Those in the work force are ambivalent. When the need for benefits is both nonexistent and remote, benefits frequently are perceived as gratuities provided by the work force. When earned income ceases because of layoff, disability, or retirement, perceptions of benefits change. Finally, those servicing the income-maintenance system view the system as providing employment, and indeed, in this part of the twentieth century the income-maintenance system is an industry.

A benefit component of the income-maintenance system (including a pension plan) of any appreciable age probably has acquired characteristics described by such words as *reward, entitlement, compensation, vested, nonforfeitable,* and *inalienable.* There is no right less susceptible to diminution than the indefeasibly vested right, and deprivation of a so-called reward invokes emotions that often have no connection with facts from the distant past. It follows that creating offsets is acrimonious.[25] Participants and beneficiaries who are organized will resist any procedure that reduces benefits, and organizations have political clout. Individual beneficiaries adversely affected by offsets will seek legal redress for loss of income, further burdening crowded court dockets. Nonetheless, if pension costs are to be manageable, offsets must be used with increasing frequency. If created carefully, they will withstand testing, for even the Supreme Court of the United States cannot be indifferent forever to the intolerable burden of runaway pension costs.

Indexing

Although *indexing*—the raising or lowering of disability or retirement benefits in accordance with some variable—is associated with inflation, adjustment of benefits occurs in the absence of inflation because perceptions of what constitutes an adequate income or an adequate standard of living change with time. For example, a pension plan providing benefits based on average income during years of service might index earned income during the earlier years of service (when income is usually lower) to yield an average that more nearly approximates earned income during the years immediately preceding retirement (when income is usually higher). Or a number of years of service at lower income might be ignored altogether in calculating the average—another means of achieving an average more nearly approximating earned income during the last years in the work force. Because the value of the American dollar has steadily declined since World War II, adjustments of this kind are related to inflation, but they also reflect an understandable desire not to require those who have participated in a general rise in the standard of living to forgo altogether their more comfortable status on leaving the work force.[26] Irrespective of whether we characterize the rewriting of a prospective pensioner's work history through indexing or adjustment, this kind of modification will continue. Only reluctantly will we concede that our standard of living is falling.

It is not getting the pensioner off to a "good start" through indexing that gives pause. It is giving him what is perceived to be an unfair advantage thereafter that raises hackles. In this connection, criticism is directed at using the consumer price index for raising retirement benefits.[27] Constructing the consumer price index includes factoring expenses not typically borne by retirees such as home-mortgage payments. Some think that, in any event, the consumer price index overstates the rise in the cost of living. To the extent that using an inappropriate index for varying pension payments results in increased benefits that are disproportionate to the rise in prices encountered by pensioners, pensioners with respect to their *pensions* (as differentiated from their *savings*) seem advantaged by inflation. And where prices rise faster than wages, using an index based on prices makes those in the work force bear a greater inflationary burden than do pensioners.

Adjustments intended to assure to a pensioner replacement income that approximates preretirement earned income when disability occurs or retirement begins should be differentiated from adjustments intended to assure that the purchasing power of replacement income remains stable. The former are directed to creating replacement income sufficient to maintain a standard of living comparable to that existing when disability occurs or retirement begins, and the latter are directed to maintaining that standard (and indeed raising it when productivity gains result in a general rise in the standard of living).

Adjustments will always be with us. For example, as our income-maintenance system matures, if we refuse to pay minimum pensions from one or more sources, we should do so as a matter of coordinating benefits from multiple pension sources, not because we have ceased to provide an income floor that approximates earned income as closely as possible. The difficulties associated with inflation can best be alleviated by ending inflation,[28] but we are not likely to end inflation quickly, if at all. That being so, we should insist on the use of adjustments appropriate to the task at hand.[29] The index used to vary pensions for the elderly might sensibly be constructed from elements different from those used to construct an index used to vary disability pensions for those in their thirties and forties. Pensioners in their thirties and forties are more likely than the elderly to be burdened with family responsibilities, including mortgages and child-education costs. They are more likely than the elderly to be heavily in debt when disability strikes. The elderly are more likely to encounter heavy hospital and medical expenses and are less likely to be burdened by transportation costs. In sum, the replacement income needs of the elderly can be differentiated from the replacement income needs of those in their middle years, and indexing should take account of that fact if the savings effected by differentiation exceed the costs of constructing and using different indexes.

Conclusion: The Prospects for Success

If we raise the normal retirement age and reduce incentives to retire early and if we restructure work to accommodate the handicapped and the elderly, can we bring into the work force some who are now dependent on the work force? Or should we assume, rather, that the advantage to be gained through such changes will originate with those already at work, and those newly entering the work force thereafter? If employees in their late forties or early fifties who are approaching or have reached the age of early retirement can be persuaded to remain in the work force, there should be little difficulty in keeping them at work. Frequently they are then at their very best—still enthusiastic, vigorous, and experienced. More important, they are presently employed and need not seek work.

Similarly, if an employee becomes disabled, we might be successful in keeping him at work if we grant disability benefits sparingly and view departure from the work force as a last resort. In the short run it might indeed be attractive to pay off the disabled rather than to rehabilitate and perhaps retrain them. But when we consider the average length of life, we cannot consider just the short run. Rehabilitation might indeed be impossible, and if so, that ends consideration of alternatives. When alternatives are realistic, we should try to keep the employee at work.

The disabled who are already outside the work force can be brought into the work force only with difficulty. The rate of unemployment in the United States is high, and it is high even if we concede that counting some as unemployed is questionable. There are many able-bodied people seeking full-time work and not finding it. If the able bodied have difficulty finding employment, many of the handicapped find it impossible to find employment, and this is true even when the handicapped are capable of performing some kinds of work, though not all.[30]

Reducing Pension Costs 145

Likewise the retired already outside the work force are not likely to be brought back into the work force in appreciable numbers. Just as there is discrimination against the handicapped in hiring, there is discrimination against the elderly in hiring, and the discrimination in hiring exists with respect to those in their forties and fifties who do not view themselves as old.[31] Legislation directed toward ending employment discrimination against the handicapped and the elderly has had little impact on hiring practices, and that state of affairs is likely to persist.

Furthermore, some pension systems are structured to discourage a pensioner from competing with those in the work force for earned income. Receipt of *unearned* income (interest, dividends) by a beneficiary of social security retirement benefits does not affect benefit levels, but receipt of earned income can. Similarly, a pensioner may find that returning to work for the employer sponsoring the pension plan from which he draws retirement benefits results in a suspension or reduction of benefits as long as he receives earned income. Where benefits payable under pension plans are suspended or reduced by earned income, pension costs are reduced on reentry of a pensioner into the work force, but the probability of reentry is low.

By way of contrast, some pension systems are structured to encourage a pensioner to remain in the work force, but his remaining in the work force will not reduce pension costs. For example, a firefighter retiring at age fifty after thirty years' service simultaneously might draw a firefighter's pension and receive earned income from a new job. The great variety in pension systems precludes assuming that keeping people in the work force or returning them to the work force will automatically reduce pension costs.

We can reduce pension costs by systematically structuring conditions of employment, including disability and retirement benefits, in such a way as to keep those already in the work force at work. Although we can try to reduce costs by bringing at least some of the retired and the disabled into the work force, our optimism on this prospect should be tempered by knowledge of the features of existing pension systems and by experience. Some of the disabled have never been in the work force. Some of the retired are completely satisfied with their situation and would reenter the work force only reluctantly. If some of the disabled and retired are nonetheless willing to seek employment, jobs are not plentiful and discrimination persists. Reducing pension costs through feasible full employment principally depends on keeping the employed at work.

Coordinating benefits to assure that replacement income does not exceed preretirement, earned income is a cost reduction device that is already a part of the income maintenance system. Coordinating benefits is not used, however, in all circumstances where it might be, and offsets encounter stiff resistance wherever efforts are made to introduce them. This state of affairs will persist, and progress in creating acceptable offsets will be slow. Progress can be hastened through increasing public awareness of the pervasive and costly nature of the income-maintenance system and awareness by the work force of the burden of support. Resistance to introduction of offsets can be softened by clear, firm assurances that devices used to limit replacement income will not be used to reduce replacement income to a point that it proves inadequate for providing the recipient with a decent standard of living.

Although neither the disabled nor the retired should bear a disproportionate share of the ill-effects of inflation, indexing their benefits to assure to them stable purchasing power should not result in their being advantaged at the expense of those still in the work force. Indexing is distasteful at best. It is relatively new to Americans, and not well understood. As we learn more about indexing, we may reasonably expect a better-informed use of indexing during this decade. Nonetheless, where an index favorable to the disabled and the retired is already in place, resistance to modification will be firm. Change will come, but it is unlikely to be summary.

Notes

1. *E.g.,* Broad, *Ending Sex Discrimination in Academia,* 208 Science 1120 (1980).

2. *See* Gilder, *The Make-Work Economy,* Harper's, Nov. 1979, at 39.

3. *See generally* Bowen, *Better Prospects for our Ailing Productivity,* Fortune, Dec. 3, 1979, at 68.

4. In describing how Mrs. Barbara Williams collected nearly $290,000 for thirty children she did not have, Los Angeles County Deputy District Attorney Ron Wheeler said, "We don't know of a bigger welfare fraud case in the history of the country." Columbus (Oh.) Citizen-Journal, June 15, 1978, at 19, cols. 1, 2.

5. *The Beneficent Monster,* Time, June 12, 1978, at 24, 26–27.

6. *See Rich New Market Among Nation's Elderly,* U.S. News & World Report, Nov. 12, 1979, at 80.

7. A majority of those retiring under social security now retire at age sixty-two rather than at age sixty-five. Social Security and Pensions: Programs of Equity and Security 21 (Staff Study, Joint Economic Committee, 96th Cong., 2d Sess., Oct. 1980). In 1950 about 80 percent of men in the age bracket sixty to sixty-four were in the work force. In 1979 the percentage had fallen to about 62 percent. *Id.* 20.

8. Congress in 1978 raised the legal mandatory-retirement age for most working Americans from sixty-five to seventy. 29 U.S.C. § 631 (Supp. 1982), *amending* 29 U.S.C. § 631 (1975).

9. An Interim Report, President's Commission on Pension Policy 46 (May 1980); *Id.* 47–48 (Nov. 1980).

10. Costa & McCrae, *Functional Age: A Conceptual and Empirical Critique,* in Second Conference on the Epidemiology of Aging 23, 44–45 [U.S. Department of Health and Human Services Publication No. (NIH) 80–969, July 1980].

11. R. Bolles, What Color is Your Parachute? 9–11 (rev. ed. 1980).

12. *See generally* Health United States 1980 271–283 [U.S. Department of Health and Human Services Publication No. (PHS) 81–1232, Dec. 1980].

13. Halloran, *Social Security Needs Long-Term Policy Changes,* OSU On Campus, Oct. 30, 1980, p. 5, col. 1.

14. Stevens, *Social Values Changed Medical System,* Columbus (Oh.) Dispatch, Mar. 15, 1981, at D2, cols. 1–6.

15. M. Carnoy & D. Shearer, Economic Democracy 170–181 (1980).

16. *See generally* R. Munts & I. Garfinkel, The Work Disincentive Effects of Unemployment Insurance 55–59 (1974); Report to the Congress by the Comptroller General, Unemployment Insurance—Inequities and Work Disincentives in the Current System i–iv (Aug. 28, 1979).

17. Kelly, *Unemployment on the Rise,* Time, Feb. 8, 1982, at 22.

18. Ginsburg, *Manpower Policy: Retrospect and Prospect,* in The Business Cycle and Public Policy 1929–1980 299, 309 (Joint Economic Committee Print 1980).

19. A retired U.S. Department of Commerce analyst reportedly was drawing an $18,000 pension while earning $25,000 from a private employer. He was quoted as saying, "I've got more money now than I ever had in my life. I figure on working at least until I'm 62. Then I'll have social security as well as a small pension from my company." Pauly & Joyce, *Poor No More,* Newsweek, Mar. 22, 1976, at 68, 70.

20. About 40 percent of retired state- and local-government employees covered by both state or local pension plans and by social security receive total retirement benefits of 100 percent to 125 percent of preretirement earnings. S. Ross, Income Security Programs: Past, Present and Future 64 (Working Paper for the President's Commission on Pension Policy, Oct. 1980).

21. Report by Working Women, National Association of Office Workers, Vanished Dreams: Age Discrimination and the Older Woman Worker 6–14 (Aug. 1980).

22. The Ethics in Government Act of 1978, Public Law 95–521, requires key federal-government personnel to make public disclosures of

their personal finances. The act is intended to reveal possible conflicts of interest.

23. Pensions are a mandatory subject of collective bargaining under *Inland Steel Company v. National Labor Relations Board,* 170 F.2d 247, 251 (7th Cir. 1948), *cert. den.,* 336 U.S. 960 (1949).

24. Deducting (offsetting) social security retirement benefits from the benefits that would otherwise be payable under a private pension plan is the simplest means of integrating benefits payable under the plan with benefits payable under social security. Schiller & Snyder, *Linkages Between Private Pensions and Social Security Reform* 7 (Information Paper Prepared for Use by the Special Committee on Aging, United States Senate, 97th Cong., 2d Sess., Apr. 1982).

25. In *Alessi v. Raybestos-Manhattan, Inc.,* and *Buczynski v. General Motors Corp.,* 451 U.S. 504 (1981), the Supreme Court held that Congress contemplated and approved pension-plan provisions providing for offsetting of workers-compensation-insurance benefits against pension retirement benefits and that such offsetting is not a violation of the nonforfeitability provisions of ERISA.

26. On congressional efforts to keep social security up to date, *see generally* Martin, *The Art of Decoupling: Keeping Social Security's Promise Up-to-Date,* 65 Cornell L. Rev. 748–800 (1980).

27. Fritz, *Is Consumer Price Index "Loaded"?,* U.S. News & World Report, Feb. 4, 1980, at 86.

28. Sloan & Miles, *Inflation Indexing—A Hair of the Dog,* Forbes, Jan. 5, 1981, at 37, 39, 42.

29. It has been suggested that a price index rather than a wage index be used to calculate initial benefits payable on retirement under social security. Ehrbar, *How to Save Social Security,* Fortune, Aug. 25, 1980, at 34, 37. *See generally* Kahn and Leveson, *How Not to Index the Economy,* Fortune, Nov. 17, 1980, at 60.

30. Davidson, *For Disabled, Jobs Few—But Many Make It,* U.S. News & World Report, Sept. 8, 1980, at 45.

31. *Discrimination Begins at 40,* Time, Feb. 2, 1981, at 81.

8
The Future of Pensions

"Will my pension be there when I need it?" That is the question thoughtful members of the work force in their thirties and forties are asking as more people become aware of what pensions are and how closely pensions are tied to the fortunes of particular businesses and entire industries, to the state of the nation's economy (including the rate of productivity and the rate of economic growth), and to changes in the population profile (including proportionately more elderly in the population as this century ends).

For those already in their fifties and early sixties contemplating retirement, the question is, "Will my retirement income be adequate?" The source of their apprehension is the situation in which some pensioners find themselves.[1] For retired persons principally dependent on social security retirement benefits for replacement income, income is barely adequate or is inadequate. Of the retired who expected private pensions to supplement social security, some are sadly disappointed. Although retired civilian and military employees of government often enjoy retirement incomes that approximate preretirement, earned incomes, employees of government are a small fraction of the work force, and government pensions are not representative of pensions in the United States. Although ideally all in the work force who can save for retirement ought to do so, Americans have no great proclivity for saving; therefore, private savings are not a significant source of retirement income.

Will pension systems persist into the next century? Did government make a fundamental mistake by encouraging the creation of pensions through the federal-income-tax deduction, exclusion, exemption, and deferral devices? Will pensions in the 1980s and 1990s permit the retired to maintain a decent standard of living—preferably a standard of living that for most of them approximates the standard of living enjoyed before retirement?

Pensions are a part of the support or income-maintenance system by which those in the work force support those who are not working—the old, the disabled, the unemployed, the young, and the poor—and those with higher incomes share with those of lower incomes or no incomes at all. The support system is chaotic, and it is hardly surprising, therefore, that the pension component of the support system is imperfect, that it all too often promises more than it delivers, and that it is being reexamined.

Because the pension systems—social security, government pensions, and private pensions—evolved at different times, in different ways, and under varying philosophies, helpful speculation on the future of pensions requires taking account of both the similarities and the differences in the pension systems.

Factors Affecting Pension Systems and Pension Benefits

The State of the Economy

The support or income-maintenance system in the United States expanded significantly after World War II during a period of prosperity interrupted only briefly by short recessions. The ambit of social security was broadened, and social security benefits were increased.[2] Local-government units without pension systems established pension plans in great numbers. Private pension plans proliferated. Expanding the income-maintenance system turned on a consensus that adequate support of the dependent segments of the population is desirable and on a willingness to share incomes to provide adequate support.

The years after World War II were years when the rate of productivity was high and increasing, when wages rose faster than prices, and when most people in the work force enjoyed a rising standard of living. Bringing in those left out of this improved state of affairs was the principal objective of the Great Society inaugurated in the mid-1960s. Sharing of incomes to eliminate poverty and alleviate suffering was economically and politically feasible because the work force was at work and times were good.

With minor exceptions, the expansion of the income-maintenance system, including pensions, was uncoordinated and unsystematic. Consequently, there is overlap, duplication, and unnecessary waste in the income-maintenance system. But in a time of general prosperity and rising expectations, inefficiency and waste were tolerable and tolerated.

Times have changed. Although no one knows the economic future of the United States, it is clear that the time of our easy superiority over the other industrial nations of the world is over. Since the mid-1960s productivity growth has declined, and the economy has slowed down. The rate of unemployment is uncomfortably high. It is far from clear that inflation has run its course.[3]

A high rate of unemployment means greater strains on unemployment-compensation systems and related parts of the income-maintenance system. High unemployment means fewer people paying social security

The Future of Pensions

taxes, which is, of course, the source of social security benefits. The unemployed are less likely than the employed to pay federal income taxes, the principal source of the federal revenues that fund federal civilian, military, and veterans pensions. High unemployment makes the employed less likely to share their incomes generously lest they too find themselves unemployed and without significant savings.

Similarly, businesses laying off workers are less likely to pay taxes as they fall due and to make periodic payments to pension funds. When businesses fail, sponsored pension plans fail.

In short, an income-maintenance system flourishes in a healthy, prosperous, expanding, productive economy. Realistically, pensions either are, or tend to be, on a pay-as-you-go basis: They depend on regular funding from the work force. A work force not wholly at work, or substantially so, has difficulty sustaining an extensive income-maintenance system, including pensions.

Funding Pension Benefits by Taxes

Social security, the most important of the pension systems, is funded by social security taxes levied directly on employees, their employers, and the self-employed. Therefore social security funds are affected directly by significant declines in employment. Nonetheless, when the unemployment rate is 10 percent, 90 percent of the work force is at work, and social security taxes are being paid. A high rate of unemployment does not have the immediate impact on social security benefits that failure of a private business has on a company-sponsored pension plan. Social security is social insurance supported by millions of working participants and backed by the promise of the federal government. A company-sponsored pension plan may involve a few hundred or a few thousand working participants and pensioners and be backed only by the Pension Benefit Guaranty Corporation (if it falls within the ambit of PBGC at all). Federal-government pension plans for civilian employees, career military personnel, and veterans are funded partially or entirely, as the case may be, from general federal revenues, principally the federal income tax. Again, when federal revenues fall, government pension benefits are less easily paid, but payment is nevertheless forthcoming. It is simply not politically feasible to withhold or appreciably reduce pensions that are funded entirely or principally from federal revenues. Social security may be bankrupt, but social security will endure. Veterans benefits are as old as the republic itself. Pensions originating with the federal government will continue to be paid in the 1980s and the 1990s.

Can the same be said of pensions originating with state and local governments? There have been recurring charges that many state- and local-government pension plans are inadequately funded, and there is some sentiment for federal regulation of public-employee retirement plans similar to that achieved through the Employee Retirement Income Security Act of 1974 (ERISA) with respect to private pension plans. Even if such legislation were enacted, it would not require immediate correction of actuarial deficiencies in state- and local-government pension plans. ERISA requires remedial funding of underfunded private pension plans over several decades. If state or local pension benefits are in jeopardy during the next twenty years, will the power of government to tax be used to assure a regular flow of benefits?

If the pension plan is a state plan rather than a local-government plan, the answer is probably yes. No government—federal, state, or local—has insisted on facing pension problems squarely, but just as the federal government is in a better position than state governments to use stop-gap financing of pension benefits, so too state governments are in a better position than local governments to manipulate funds to assure an uninterrupted flow of benefits. Pensioners of small local-government units are like pensioners of weak private pension plans. They are vulnerable to drastic changes in the economic environment that funds their source of retirement income.

The power to tax affects not only the regular flow of retirement benefits but also the adequacy of benefits. Generally speaking, federal-government pensioners (as differentiated from social security beneficiaries) are the elite of the retired. Their initial benefits are more generous than those paid to other pensioners, and they are advantaged by periodic increases in benefits to offset the rising cost of living. As compared to participants in private pension plans, participants in state- and local-government pension plans are similarly advantaged, but the advantages are much less striking. Nearly all federal civilian employees fall under a single pension system. There are innumerable state- and local-government pension plans, and the great variety of plans permits variation in the characteristics and quality of pensions from state to state and within states.

Early Retirement and Mandatory Retirement

When the average length of life was shorter than it is today, most people who entered the work force worked throughout life. Until social security was adopted in the mid-1930s, few Americans were covered by pension plans.

During the years after World War II, withdrawal from the work force because of age became a realistic goal for an ever-increasing share of the work force as the ambit of social security was broadened and private pension plans proliferated. Governments at all levels increased the numbers of their employees, making them participants in existing or newly created government pension plans. And retirement at what was considered the normal retirement age of sixty-five or seventy was gradually complemented by early retirement at age sixty-two (under social security) or even fifty-five or sixty (under government or private pension plans).[4]

People still in the work force in their fifties, sixties, and early seventies are not dependent on the work force for support. Indeed, they are helping to support others. The fewer pensioners there are, the less strain there is on pension systems. Clearly, it is in the public interest that people in the work force continue to work as long as feasible.

Although we can expect some limited success in inducing older people to remain at work, normal retirement at age sixty-five or seventy has been with us for several generations of workers, and it is unlikely that significant changes will be observed soon in the normal retirement age. Early retirement is a much more recent notion, and as the burden of supporting the retired becomes better understood, the work force is likely to insist that early retirement be used only when it is clearly in the public interest to indulge it. To the extent that early retirement becomes exceptional, pension systems are advantaged.

Mandatory or compulsory retirement has fallen into disrepute and is undergoing reexamination. But were it to disappear altogether, its effect on pension systems would not necessarily be appreciable. For most working Americans the legal mandatory retirement age is seventy. Although there are many people in their seventies in good health, capable of work and willing to work, we do not know what the total number of such people is. In contrast, the effect of early retirement on pension systems has been documented.[5]

Calculating Benefits

After World War II, wages rose faster than prices, and there was a rise in the American standard of living. To some extent the dependent segments of the population shared that improved standard of living with the work force. In particular, those withdrawing from the work force because of disability or age shared through calculation of benefits in a way that reflected general prosperity and rising wage scales.[6] Where an average of annual earnings entered into the calculation, low wages characteristically earned during the earlier years of employment might be indexed to reflect changes in wage scales that occurred over time. Some earlier years of low earnings might be disregarded altogether. As an alternative to an average arrived at through taking account of all, or substantially all, of the years in the work force, an average arrived at by taking account of a few years (say, five or three) of highest earnings might be used. The period of service entering into the calculation of benefits might be lengthened appreciably by giving credit for similar work elsewhere, or for military service (including military service that did not in fact interrupt work, however disagreeable the service might have been). Through such strategies, people retiring in the 1950s and thereafter were accorded disability and retirement benefits that more closely approximated preretirement earned incomes than would have been the case absent such strategies.

Although it is difficult to fault calculating benefits in a way that permits all dependent people to share in a rising standard of living, calculation of benefits affects both the level of pension benefits and total pension payouts. Methods of calculation that are heavily relied on by prospective beneficiaries are not likely to be revised immediately, but reexamination will occur as the cry to reduce pension costs becomes more insistent.

Coordination of Benefits (Offsets)

Because nearly everyone in the private work force falls under social security, a private employer creating a private pension plan might sensibly coordinate social security benefits and private pension plan benefits by integrating the two. To qualify for favorable federal-income-tax treatment under the Internal Revenue Code, a private pension plan that integrates benefits must do so in a way that does not discriminate in favor of employees who are highly paid. About one-third of all private pension plan participants fall under integrated pension plans.[7]

Although nine out of every ten people with earned incomes fall under social security, federal employees other than those in the armed forces do not, and many state- and local-government employees do not. But federal-, state-, and local-government employees who do not fall under social security through their government employment might nonetheless at some time accumulate social security quarters of coverage through other careers or part-time employment. On withdrawal from the work force, they might qualify for pensions from multiple sources, and unlike pensioners of integrated private pension plans, they do not find themselves drawing benefits from pension programs that systematically anticipate coordination of benefits.

Although the work force provides retirement incomes that approach or approximate preretirement, earned incomes, it is unlikely that an informed work force will provide retirement incomes that exceed preretirement, earned incomes. Coordinating benefits *(offsetting)* is a controversial, acrimonious means of reducing pension costs, but it unquestionably will be resorted to as the pension burden becomes less tolerable. For the minority of participants entitled to benefits from multiple sources, offsetting will result in a disagreeable reduction in total benefits.

The Dependency Ratio

Viewed from the standpoint of those withdrawing from the work force in the 1980s and 1990s, the population profile is not ideal, and the low fertility rate gives pause, but nonetheless the work force is large when compared to the number of people aged sixty-five or more, and it includes an important group—the baby-boom generation born in the fifteen years after World War II when 64 million children were born. The older among the parents of these children are retiring, and they can take some comfort in the knowledge that the large number of children they raised makes somewhat less burdensome to each member of the work force the economic cost entailed in supporting the old.

There are now five people of working age for each person aged sixty-five or more—a favorable "dependency ratio."[8] (People aged sixty-five or more are usually out of the work force,[9] and are dependent on the work force.) Because the fertility rate has fallen, because the baby-boom generation will itself age, and because the effect of net immigration cannot be predicted with certainty, there might be only three people of working age for each person aged sixty-five or more by the third decade of the next century. And the working will be supporting not only themselves and the old but also the young, the unemployed, the disabled, and the poor.

Although the dependency ratio is presently favorable, it is clear that it will become less so. It is possible, of course, that a remarkable technological breakthrough will enable great masses of Americans to forgo work altogether and simply contemplate the human condition. Just as automation twenty years ago was to give us unexpected leisure, now robotics is to do so. But we cannot count on that. When the burden of support is widely diffused, it can and does persist for years unnoticed except by a few. When the burden is transferred to a group growing proportionately smaller with every passing year, it gets attention. An unfavorable dependency ratio will require that the chaotic income-maintenance system be restructured to bring inefficiency and waste to an irreducible minimum.

Costs of Administering Pension Systems

Pension systems require the collection of funds from which to pay benefits, the identification of beneficiaries, the calculation of benefits, and the disbursement of funds. If a system is *funded,* investment of accumulated funds occurs. The proliferation of pension plans that was a part of the post-World War II expansion of the support or income-maintenance system gave rise to what is not unfairly styled a "pension industry"[10]—that is, a preponderatingly white-collar service group consisting of accountants, actuaries, lawyers, bankers, insurers, investment counselors, administrators, and clerks who assist in creating and processing pension benefits. This service group is an important part of the work force, and its emergence accounts for part of the great increase in service jobs that occurred in the 1960s and 1970s.

Both pension benefits and the administrative costs of servicing pension plans are paid for by the work force. To the extent that having numerous pension plans causes unnecessary duplication of administrative tasks, with concomitant duplication of costs, funds available for pension benefits are reduced. But reducing duplication of tasks causes reduction of incomes and loss of jobs, neither of which carries popular appeal. Nonetheless, as the pension systems mature and the support burden becomes proportionately heavier, some duplication of tasks will disappear as part of the effort to keep administrative costs reasonable. Our preference for pluralism and diversity in pension systems requires some loss in efficiency. It does not require waste.

Other Components of the Income-Maintenance System

Although for the elderly, pension systems are the most important element in the support system, they are but one element. Pensions are payable in money, and money gives access to goods and services. If needed goods or services are provided in kind, that reduces the strain put on a modest pension.

Among the in-kind benefits available to the retired elderly are health care (principally but not exclusively through medicare and medicaid) and housing. But there are other types of in-kind assistance that are of some importance. Numerous food, recreation, and transportation benefits are available to the elderly. It bears emphasis, however, that the availability of in-kind services is different from the regular receipt of a pension check by mail. The U.S. Postal Service prides itself on reaching addressees in remote or inhospitable areas. Some of the elderly never profit from in-kind benefits because the benefits realistically are beyond their reach. Furthermore, if an in-kind benefit is available but not needed (health care, for example), it is worth something, but it is difficult to value as income.

If every pension system were to pay pension benefits permitting beneficiaries to maintain a decent standard of living, in-kind benefits would become more closely identified with their principal justification—assisting the very poor.[11] Because there is great variation in pension benefits, in-kind benefits cannot be disregarded altogether in assessing the factors that bear on total pension payments and the level of pension benefits. For lying behind some pension systems is the unstated assumption that if need be, pension benefits will be supplemented by one or more of the other elements in the income-maintenance system. That is certainly so with respect to social security, and it is all too frequently so with respect to private pension plans.

Investment Experience

Where accumulation of pension funds requires investment, managers of institutional funds, including pension plan funds, have shared in the difficulties encountered by individuals in trying to invest profitably. To the extent that investments earn income, pension plans are advantaged. If a funded pension plan has existed for several decades and funding has been adequate and uninterrupted, profitable investments contribute significantly to pension payments, and occasionally are used to justify ad hoc increases in the benefits of those already retired. There is a move now afoot to use pension funds to reindustrialize the United States or to provide mortgage money to revitalize the depressed housing industry. Such social investing requires changes in the existing legal constraints on investment of pension funds. If social investing causes lower returns on investments than would obtain in the absence of social investing, social investing in the short run adversely affects pension costs.

Labor Mobility and Wage Levels

The level of pension benefits is usually arrived at by taking account of both the span of covered employment and the wage or salary earned. Americans change jobs frequently. Although mobility has no effect on continuity of coverage under social security, it can preclude qualifying for benefits under private pension plans and government pension plans. Indeed, the expected failure of some workers to qualify for retirement benefits is forthrightly factored in during construction of pension plans. Mobility is highly prized, and the solution to qualifying workers for pension-plan benefits does not lie in tying them to a particular employer. It lies in such notions as early vesting, portability, and reciprocity. Until these notions become fully developed, labor mobility will affect pension costs and levels of benefits.

Disparities in pension benefits reflect the disparities in earned incomes in the United States. During their working lives, some Americans enjoy high incomes and others never earn more than subsistence wages. High incomes are said to be essential to attracting the best-qualified talent. Money unquestionably is a factor in attracting talent. But just as it will not do to assess the adequacy of retirement benefits payable in money without taking account of various in-kind benefits available to the elderly, so too it will not do to look at money alone when considering the factors that induce people to seek and take work. Once an adequate level of income in money has been attained, some people are attracted to work by the opportunity to exercise power or by other indicia of success (a lavish office, generous expense accounts, presence of sycophants in appropriate numbers, conspicuous traveling, extended vacations, and the like).

In 1981, a year when American companies sought—and obtained—so-called givebacks from organized labor, executive compensation rose by more than 10 percent.[12] The top officers of two dozen corporations have annual incomes exceeding $1 million.[13] Disparities in income exist in all societies. Soviet leaders have their dachas and Soviet workers have their two-room apartments. Disparities in income are defensible; embarrassing disparities are not.[14] The largest bulge in the American population, the baby-boom generation born after World War II, brought to maturity during a period of general prosperity and rising expectations, sent to colleges and universities in numbers both absolutely and proportionately greater than ever before, finds itself seeking fulfillment in a period of economic decline. If it finds opportunities for advancement foreclosed by the sheer number of qualified applicants, will it seek higher pay scales for the numerous people who must settle for work at a level well below that to which they aspire? If so, will that carry with it a real rise in wages for those working at the bottom of the pay scale? And will incomes at the top fall precipitously as cutting the economic pie is politicized? If convergence of incomes occurs and the average wage rises, pension costs and retirement-benefit levels ultimately will reflect the change.

The Work Place

Pension benefits are payable on leaving the work force because of disability or age. To the extent that the workplace can be made safe and healthful, and work itself made less distasteful, workers are more likely to remain with the same employer, disability is less likely to occur, and both early retirement and normal retirement become less attractive. Improving the workplace is the purpose of the controversial Occupational Safety and Health Act adopted by Congress in 1970. People at work are not being supported by others, and it is in the public interest that working conditions encourage the work force to remain at work.

Only a fortunate few in the work force find their work a constant joy. Most work includes some drudgery, and it is foolish to think that the work force can free itself altogether from distasteful work. The most that we realistically can hope for is improvement in working conditions significant enough to induce the work force to remain at work as long as work is feasible.

Suggestions for changing the nature of work include redesigning work,[15] introducing *flex-time* (variation in the hours of starting and stopping work), using a much higher proportion of part-time workers, granting generous maternity and paternity leaves, giving longer vacations with pay, granting extended leaves of absence without pay (but without loss of such important fringe benefits as group life and health insurance), and including worker participation in decision making.[16]

Improving the quality of working life (QWL) is related to improving the rate of productivity. Although government, business, and labor generally are agreed that the rate of productivity should be improved, there is no agreement on how to go about it.[17] Traditionally, American management and labor have been adversaries. Improving the quality of working life requires cooperation. Whether that cooperation will be forthcoming is not clear. If the quality of working life improves significantly and workers remain on the job, strains on pension plans are reduced.

Conclusion

Pensions are one of a number of methods by which the work force supports the disabled and the retired. They are part of the income-transfer (transfer-payments) system by which those with higher incomes share with those of lower incomes or no incomes at all. They are also a part of the wealth-transmission system.[18] Through pension systems, the head of a household frequently (but not always) provides for his surviving spouse and dependent children. Under some circumstances, a participant's interest in a pension system passes at death to his successors in interest in much the same fashion that a participant's interest in a bank account or a life-insurance policy passes. That is, to the extent that participation in a pension plan is a form of forced saving, a participant's interest in a pension plan is property, with the characteristics that property has.[19] But pension systems differ from more conventional property devices in that they facilitate not only transfers *from* the participant to his spouse (conventionally viewed as in the same generation as that of the participant) and to his dependents (who are in the generation younger than that of the participant) but also transfers *to* the participant from the younger generations still in the work force. Although some pension systems include the accumulation of substantial assets, all pension systems are heavily dependent on a regular flow of funds from those in the work force in order to assure a regular flow of benefits to the disabled, the retired, and their survivors and dependents. This paradoxical state of affairs originates in the mixed nature of many pension systems—they include both the element of forced saving (represented by accumulation of assets) and the element of social contract (represented by regular funding from the work force to assure the payment of benefits at levels that cannot be sustained for any appreciable length of time from accumulated assets and earnings alone).

All property devices change with time, and pension systems will change. Pension systems are affected by an array of circumstances, including both the obvious (for example, retirement patterns)[20] and the less apparent (for example, the dependency ratio). How will pension systems evolve during the 1980s and 1990s? Will they look much the same in the year 2010 as they look today?

Pension systems are not likely to change appreciably in the next decade. Resistance to significant modification is enormous. The retired are numerous, vociferous, and militant. If their position on modification is reasonable, they easily find reasoned support. If their position is unreasonable, demagogs rush to their aid. During the 1980s and 1990s, a large share of the retired will consist of veterans of World War II—an identifiable group with a double claim to special consideration. The political climate for significant change is simply not propitious.

Nonetheless, changes in pensions will be discussed, and some will get underway. Unless the economy booms (so that the burden of support is relatively tolerable), the age of early retirement will be raised and the benefit incentives for early retirement will be made less attractive. Calculation of benefits will be reconsidered to try to assure that the financial burdens of periods of economic stress are borne about equally by those in the work force and those who have withdrawn from the work force. Coordination of benefits (offsetting) to foreclose retirement benefits that exceed preretirement earned income will slowly be instituted, first with respect to pension systems that are public and ultimately with respect to those that are quasi-public (private). The extent to which offsetting occurs will turn on how heavy the work force perceives the pension burden to be, and how successful the retired are in invoking legal and emotional bars to the offsetting process.

The economic difficulties of the early 1980s have made clear the close tie between a healthy, growing, productive economy and the pension systems. The economic decline of parts of the heavily industrialized Midwest and Northeast underlies the call for reindustrialization of the United States. Road, bridges, dams, waterways, sewers, and water and fuel lines need replacement and repair. Replacing old factories, introducing new machinery, and upgrading the infrastructure require outlay of vast sums of money. Accumulated pension funds are viewed as a likely source of financing the economic recovery of the country.[21] Attempts to change the law on investment of pension funds to accommodate pressure groups seeking new sources of money will occur with increasing frequency, and some changes in the law will be made.

Although the President's Commission on Pension Policy recommended compulsory minimum universal pension coverage as an unintegrated supplement to social security,[22] there is little evidence that the recommendation will be seriously considered. Creating a Minimum Universal Pension System (MUPS) for workers in both government and private employment would be a major undertaking, one not easily proposed when the work force looks on social security as the government-sponsored source of disability and retirement benefits to replace earned income. That the work force has imperfect knowledge of the purpose of social security (to serve as an income floor) is in this connection irrelevant. We believe what we prefer to believe, and Americans prefer to believe that social security is a comprehensive system of social insurance.

The deficiencies in retirement benefits originate both in the pension systems and in the workplace. It is generally agreed that retirement benefits from all sources should approximate preretirement, earned income but should not exceed earned income. Coordination of benefits can be anticipated in constructing a pension plan, but a plan cannot require wage levels high enough to assure retirement benefits that approximate preretirement, earned income. Similarly, a pension plan can altogether ignore (wisely or not) the difference in longevity of men and women, but a plan cannot require that women be represented in jobs at all wage levels in proportion to their numbers in the work force. Women are a permanent part of the work force,[23] but they enter and leave the work force more frequently than men, they frequently work part time, and they earn low wages—none of which is conducive to qualifying for a satisfactory level of retirement benefits. Neither mothers nor fathers who spend full time caring for their small children accumulate pension credits for doing so. Generally speaking, qualifying for a good pension requires being uninterruptedly at work, at a good wage, over an appreciable number of years, under a good pension plan. Some Americans are fortunate enough to find themselves in such circumstances. Many fall short of doing so, and their lower retirement benefits reflect that fact. Some Americans never qualify for retirement benefits at all.

This situation will continue, for the workplace in the United States changes slowly. If the quality of working life were to improve significantly, the work force might be induced to remain at work substantially throughout life, and dependency on pension systems would decline. If the rate of productivity were to rise, disparities in wage levels might narrow, and retirement-benefit levels ultimately would reflect the change. We can hope for both but should count on neither.[24]

The income-maintenance system is firmly entrenched; it will not be abandoned. But if the system is not to be a continuing source of waste, conflict, and bickering, it must be improved. Disability and retirement pensions are significant parts of the income-maintenance system. Costs of providing pensions have increased remarkably in a short period of time, and costs are out of hand. Costs can be reduced in a number of ways. It is unquestionably true that some cost-cutting devices are less politically acceptable than others, and some create difficult legal problems. But raising the established retirement age and deemphasizing early retirement are not revolutionary ideas. Coordinating benefits is controversial but not novel. Indexing can be mastered. Therefore, let us get on with the task of cutting pension costs. Not in 1990, not in 2000, but now.

Notes

1. E. Meier & C. Dittmar, Income of the Retired, Levels and Sources i (Working Paper for the President's Commission on Pension Policy, Oct. 1980).

2. B. Stein, Social Security and Pensions in Transition 50–60 (1980).

3. When both the rate of inflation and the rate of unemployment are high, the condition is described as *stagflation*. Dernburg, *Stagflation: Causes and Cures,* in Stagflation: The Causes, Effects and Solutions, Joint Economic Committee, 96th Cong., 2d Sess., 1 (Dec. 1980).

4. *See generally* E. Meier & C. Dittmar, Varieties of Retirement

Ages 1–13 (Working Paper for the President's Commission on Pension Policy, Jan. 1980).

5. Voluntary Early Retirement in the Civil Service Too Often Misused 23–25 (Report to the Congress by the Comptroller General of the United States, Dec. 31, 1980).

6. On the shift toward adequacy of social security benefits, *see* M. Derthick, Policymaking for Social Security 213–227 (1979).

7. Schiller & Snyder, *Linkages Between Private Pensions and Social Security Reform* 7 (Information Paper Prepared for Use by the Special Committee on Aging, United States Senate, 97th Cong., 2d Sess., Apr. 1982).

8. Human Resources and Demographics: Characteristics of People and Policy 19 (Staff Study, Joint Economic Committee, 96th Cong., 2d Sess., Nov. 1980).

9. Of those sixty-five and older, 92 percent of the women and 80 percent of the men are out of the work force. E. Meier & C. Dittmar, Varieties of Retirement Ages iv (Working Paper for the President's Commission on Pension Policy, Jan. 1980).

10. J. Gollin, The Star Spangled Retirement Dream 50–83 (1981).

11. T. Borzilleri, In-Kind Benefit Programs and Retirement Income i (Working Paper for the President's Commission on Pension Policy, Oct. 1980).

12. Pauly & Ipsen, *The Cream at the Top,* Newsweek, May 17, 1982, at 76.

13. Wingo & Morse, *Executives' Pay Goes Up, Up, and Away,* U.S. News & World Report, May 24, 1982, at 59, 60.

14. *See generally* Loomis, *The Madness of Executive Compensation,* Fortune, July 12, 1982, at 42; Thurow, *The Widening Income Gap,* Newsweek, Oct. 5, 1981, at 70.

15. *See* Oldham, *Work Redesign,* 62 Nat. Forum, The Phi Kappa Phi J. 8 (1982).

16. *See* Kanter, *Dilemmas of Participation,* 62 Nat. Forum, The Phi Kappa Phi J. 16 (1982).

17. Gendron, *The Great Productivity Scam,* 62 Nat. Forum, The Phi Kappa Phi J. 24 (1982).

18. *See generally* Chapter 4 *supra,* Pensions in the Changing Wealth Transmission Process, at 65.

19. An interest in a pension plan is likely to be subject to a spendthrift restraint. *See,* for example, 29 U.S.C. § 1056(d) (1975), with respect to private pension plans falling under ERISA.

20. *See* E. Meier & C. Dittmar, Varieties of Retirement Ages 14–51 (Working Paper for the President's Commission on Pension Policy, Jan. 1980).

21. *See* Final Report [California] Governor's Public Investment Task Force ix–xi (Oct. 1981).

22. Coming of Age: Toward a National Retirement Income Policy 1 (Final Report, President's Commission on Pension Policy, Feb. 26, 1981).

23. A. Kessler-Harris, Out to Work 300–301 (1982).

24. The share of aggregate income (before taxes but after transfer payments) of the poorest 20 percent and the second-poorest 20 percent of Americans is said to have changed little over the last fifty years. J. Hochschild, What's Fair? 3 (1981).

Glossary

Although some pension terms have acquired a generally accepted definition or a definition that is confined to a particular context, many are used in an imprecise way. The meanings set out below are intended to assist in general reading or discussion; they do not necessarily apply in every context.

Accrual of benefits. The process of accumulating pension credits or pension funds for a participant in a pension plan.

Actuarial assumptions. Factors used by actuaries in determining the costs of a pension plan. Examples of such factors are mortality rates among participants in a pension plan, turnover rate among employees because of death or job termination, rate of return on pension plan investments, and rate of wage inflation.

Annuitant. One who receives an annuity. See also Annuity.

Annuity. A contract providing an income for a number of years or for the life of the person receiving the payment (the annuitant); the payment received under the contract; a pension. See also Variable annuity.

Beneficiary. A participant in a pension or health-and-welfare plan; a person designated by a participant or by the terms of a plan to receive a benefit based on the eligibility of the participant. See also Participant.

Break in service. A period during which a person who would otherwise be a participant in a pension plan is not accumulating pension credits or pension funds because of a temporary cessation of covered employment.

Cash-out. A lump-sum payment to a participant of his nonforfeitable interest on terminating employment before retirement.

Claimant. A person with a claim to a benefit under a pension plan. See also Participant.

Contributory plan. A pension plan in which participants contribute to the fund that is the source of pension payments. See also Noncontributory plan.

Coverage. A definition of what benefits are available, to whom, in accordance with what conditions, under a pension or health-and-welfare plan.

Covered employee. A participant in a pension plan who is currently employed. See also Participant.

Credited service. A period of employment that is recognized for purposes of eligibility for pension payments or for purposes of fixing the level of pension payments.

Credits. The interest of a participant in a pension plan based on contributions by him or on his behalf and on the period of such contributions.

Current value. See Present value.

Death benefit. Lump-sum payment made upon the death of a participant.

Defined-benefit plan. A pension plan in which pensions are established in advance by a formula and contributions to the plan vary. A *flat benefit* is a specified amount per month payable at retirement; a *fixed benefit* is a stated percentage of compensation; a *unit benefit* is a stated percentage of compensation multiplied by years of service. See also Defined-contribution plan.

Defined-contribution plan. A pension plan in which contributions to an individual account for each participant are made by employer or employee or both in accordance with a formula, and the pension payable varies. See also Defined-benefit plan.

Disability benefit. See Disability pension.

Disability pension. Periodic payments made to a participant who becomes permanently disabled before the time of normal retirement under a pension plan.

Discounted value. See Present value.

Disqualified person. People listed in the federal-tax law who are closely connected with the creation and administration of a pension plan; a party in interest. See also Prohibited transactions.

Double-dipping. Drawing similar benefits from more than one public source of payments.

Early retirement. Retirement at an age earlier than normal retirement age under a pension plan (for example, retirement at age fifty-five under a plan calling for normal retirement at age seventy).

Eligibility requirements. Conditions that one must meet to participate in a pension plan or to qualify for pension benefits.

Employee benefit plan. See Pension plan; see Welfare plan.

Employee Retirement Income Security Act (ERISA). An act (popularly called ERISA or the pension-reform act) passed by Congress in 1974 to try to assure pensions to participants in qualified private pension plans.

Forfeiture. Loss of nonvested pension credits on terminating employment prior to retirement.

Funded plan. A pension plan in which pensions are payable from accumulated funds (whether insured or trusteed) rather than paid as a current operating expense. See also Unfunded plan.

Health plan. See Welfare plan.

H.R. 10 plan. See Keogh plan.

Indexing. Adjusting pension payments in accordance with a variable such as the consumer price index.

Individual Retirement Account (IRA). A qualified pension plan primarily for (but not restricted to) an employed person not otherwise covered by a qualified pension plan or a government pension plan. See also Keogh plan.

Insured. A participant in an insured pension plan; a participant in the social security system who has accumulated a specified number of credits.

Insured plan. A pension plan under which pension payments are made by an insurance company that administers the plan. See also Trusteed plan.

Integration. The dovetailing of pension benefits under one plan with those under another plan; the dovetailing of pension benefits under a private pension plan with pension benefits under social security.

Investment return. The yield on investment of pension funds.

Joint and survivor annuity. An annuity providing payments as long as either of two persons is alive; an annuity payable to husband and wife. See also Annuity.

Keogh plan. A qualified pension plan established by a self-employed person.

Lump-sum payment. Payment within one taxable year of the entire balance payable to a participant of a qualified pension or employee annuity plan.

Mortality rate. The proportion of the number of deaths in a group of persons to the number of persons in the group at the beginning of the period during which the deaths occur.

Multiemployer plan. A pension plan to which more than one employer contributes.

Noncontributory plan. A pension plan funded solely by an employer (or group of employers). See also Contributory plan.

OASDI. Old age, survivors, and disability insurance—commonly called "social security."

Offset. Reduction in benefits because of payments receivable by the participant or beneficiary from some other source deemed duplicative.

Participant. Person participating in the pension plan (a covered current employee or retired former employee). See also Beneficiary.

Party in interest. Persons listed in federal law on fiduciary administration who are closely connected with the creation and administration of a pension plan; a disqualified person. See also Prohibited transactions.

Past service cost. The part of current pension cost attributable to liability for pension payments based in part on the period of a participant's employment that preceded creation of the pension plan. See also Past service credit.

Past service credit. Pension credit restored to a participant in a plan who had earned credit and then withdrawn it on termination of employment; pension credit accorded to a participant in a plan for a period of employment occurring while not a participant. See also Past service cost.

Pension assets. See Pension funds.

Pension Benefit Guaranty Corporation (PBGC). A corporation established under the Employee Retirement Income Security Act of 1974 (ERISA) to insure participants in defined-benefit, qualified pension plans against loss of pensions on termination of a plan.

Pension funds. Property (including securities) bought with contributions from employers or employees (or both), and accumulations of income from the property.

Pension liabilities. The total obligation to pay pensions to participants during the life of the pension plan.

Pension plan. A plan established to provide income upon retirement from the work force because of age or disability.

Pension Reform Act. See Employee Retirement Income Security Act.

Plan population. Participants still in the work force, retired participants, participants terminated with vested rights (former employees), spouses and other dependents of retired and deceased participants.

Portability. Transferability of pension credits upon change of employment by a participant.

Present value. The discounted value (that is, the current-dollar value) of payments receivable in the future.

Prior service credit. See Past service credit.

Prohibited transaction. Activities impermissible for fiduciaries under federal law. See also Disqualified person.

Prudent-man rule. A rule applied to judge the propriety of investment of trust funds. The rule has been made federal with respect to qualified pension plans by the Employee Retirement Income Security Act of 1974 (ERISA).

Qualified plan. A pension plan that is constructed and administered to qualify for tax advantages under the Internal Revenue Code.

Rollover. The transfer of funds from one qualified plan to another without loss of tax advantages under the Internal Revenue Code.

Social security. See OASDI.

Transferability. See Portability.

Trusteed plan. A pension plan in which accumulated pension funds are administered by a trustee (or trustees). See also Insured plan.

Turnover rate. The rate at which participants quit jobs, are fired, or in some other way end their employment (and hence affect their eligibility for pensions or other benefits).

Unfunded-pension liabilities. That part of the total obligation to pay pensions that is not covered by accumulated pension funds. See also Pension liabilities.

Unfunded plan. A pension plan in which pensions are payable from current revenues. See also Funded plan.

Variable annuity. An annuity in which the amount payable varies according to investment experience. See also Annuity.

Vested benefits. A right to a pension that is not dependent on continuing employment by a participant until retirement age.

Welfare plan. A plan that provides medical, surgical, dental, or hospital benefits under specified circumstances.

Index

Aid to families with dependent children, 24
Aliens. *See* Immigration
Annuity, 2–3, 41; fixed, 2; indexed, 2; variable, 2
Automation, 1, 19

Baby-boom generation, 18–20, 27
Bank accounts, 73; custodial, 73; joint, 73; pay-on-death, 73; Totten trust, 73
Blanketing in, 6
Breaks in service, 89–90

Capital, 30, 31, 104; need for, 30; and pension funds, 104
Charity, 65, 74, 80–81; contemporary purposes, 74; policing, 80–81; shift from, 74; and third sector, 74
Children, 24, 67–69; care of, 68–70; and divorce, 67–68; illegitimate, 24; rights of, 68; support for, 24, 44, 65, 68
Civil-service retirement system. *See* Federal civil-service pensions; State- and local-government pensions
Common ownership, 74–75
Community property, 56, 75; and pension rights, 56
Compulsory retirement. *See* Retirement age
Coordination of benefits. *See* Offsets
Costs. *See* Pension costs
CSRS. *See* Federal civil-service pensions

Demography, 17–28; blacks, 23, 24, 25; children, 23, 24; disabled, 24–25; elderly, 23, 24; females, 23, 27–28; Hispanics, 23; illegitimates, 24; males, 23; and pension crunch, 17; poor, 26; population profile, 17–18; total population, 22; unemployed, 25–26; veterans, 24; whites, 23, 24, 25; work force, 26–28
Dependency ratio, 27, 155–156. *See also* Demography
Disability pensions, 45, 48, 99–100
Disabled, 24–25; support for, 25, 45, 48, 99–100
Double-dipping, 6–7, 101–103, 137–140; and social security, 7, 53, 56, 57, 102. *See also* Offsets

Early retirement. *See* Retirement age
Economic Recovery Tax Act of 1981, 41
Elderly, 23–24; number of, 31; support for, 24
Employee Retirement Income Security Act of 1974, 10–11, 41, 85–97; breaks in service under, 89–90; and church plans, 85, 97; conflict of interest under, 93–94; and contingent employer liability insurance, 96; disclosure and reporting under, 95–96; fiduciary conduct under, 93–94; funding requirements of, 94–95; and government plans, 85, 97; joint and survivor annuity under, 92; participation requirements under, 90–91; Pension Benefit Guaranty Corporation created, 96; and portability of credits, 86, 92; preemption by, 86–87; prohibited transactions under, 93–94; prudent-man rule adopted, 93; service requirements under, 90–91; state and local law, preemption by, 86–87; and surviving spouse, 91–92; vesting schedules of, 86, 88
ERISA. *See* Employee Retirement Income Security Act of 1974

171

ERTA. *See* Economic Recovery Tax Act of 1981

Family, 65–71; children, 67–69; and divorce, 66–67; grandparents, 70–71; spouse, 66
Federal civil-service pensions, 4, 15, 41, 52–53, 151; adequacy, 53; dependents benefits, 53; and double-dipping, 53; and social security, 53; spouse's benefits, 53
Fertility rate, 20–21
Food stamps, 42, 47
Forfeitures, 12
Future of pensions, 149–159; and calculating benefits, 153–154; and compulsory retirement, 153; and coordinating benefits, 154–155; and the dependency ratio, 155–156; and disparities in earned incomes, 158; and early retirement, 152–153; and the economy, 150–151; and the federal government, 151; in-kind benefits, 156–157; and investment experience, 157; and labor mobility, 157–158; and normal retirement, 153; and offsets, 154–155; and service costs, 156; and state- and local-government, 151–152; and taxation, 151–152; and the work place, 159

Generation, 27; baby-boom, 18–20, 27
Guaranteed annual income, 1

Immigration, 22; aliens, 22; illegal, 22; legal, 22; net, 22
Income disparities, 19–20, 158
Income maintenance system, 1–2, 10–13, 15–17, 42–57, 60, 127, 150, 156–157, 162; civil service pensions, 15, 52–53; medicaid, 15; medicare, 15; military pensions, 15, 55–56; and pension plans, 15; private pensions, 15, 48–52; railroaders pensions, 15, 57; social security, 15, 42–48; state- and local-government pensions, 53–55; supplemental security income, 15; unemployment compensation, 15, 26; veterans pensions, 15, 57; workers' compensation, 15
Income tax, 16, 41, 86
Income transfers, 5–6, 41, 61; and pensions, 5, 61
Indexing, 5, 142–144; and consumer price index, 5, 143; federal pensions, 5; private pensions, 52; state- and local-government pensions, 5
Individual retirement account, 41, 73, 85, 86, 87–88; contribution to, 87; distribution of, 87; and rollover, 87; for spouse, 87
Inflation, 97–98
Infrastructure, 31, 161; and pension funds, 161; repair of, 161
Institutional investors, 121
Investing pension funds, 52, 104, 112–123, 157; and AFL-CIO, 111; and duty of loyalty, 114; under ERISA, 112–113, 114, 115; by institutional investors, 111–112; and Internal Revenue Code, 120; legal constraints, 112–119; under noncontributory plans, 120; NYC Teachers' Retirement System, 117; and participants, 119–121; political constraints, 119–121; and prudent-man rule, 112–113; for social purposes, 113–119; sums involved, 121; Taft-Hartley act, 113, 114; and United Mine Workers of America, 116–117
Investments. *See* Investing pension funds
IRA. *See* Individual retirement account

Keogh plan, 73

Index

Life expectancy, 21–22, 41; blacks, 22; females, 22; males, 22; whites, 22
Life insurance, 72–73; to create estate, 73

Mandatory retirement. *See* Retirement age
Medicaid, 15
Medicare, 15
Military pensions, 4, 15, 41, 55–56, 151; adequacy, 56; for career military personnel, 56; and social security, 55–56
Mortality rate, 21–22
Mortality tables, 17

Negative income tax, 1

Offsets, 12, 101–102, 138–142, 154–155; creating, 140–142; under social security, 101–102
Old age, survivors, and disability insurance. *See* Social security

PBGC. *See* Pension Benefit Guaranty Corporation
Pension. *See* Annuity
Pension Benefit Guaranty Corporation, 50, 78, 85, 95–97
Pension costs, 127–144, 156; and consumer price index, 143; and coordination of benefits, 137–142; and early retirement, 128, 135–136; and full employment, 127–137; and indexing, 142–144; and mandatory retirement, 131; and normal retirement, 131–135; and offsets, 140–142
Pension crunch, 17, 32. *See also* Demography; Dependency ratio
Pension funds, 8; and institutional investors, 8, 52, 104; insured, 3, 8; investing, 8, 52, 104, 112–123; trusteed, 3, 8
Pension plans, 3–4, 58–61, 78–80; assets of, 8; contributory, 3; criticisms of, 9–10; defined benefit, 4, 50; defined contribution, 4, 50; federal civil-service, 4, 15, 41, 52–53; and government involvement, 58–59, 78; and income maintenance system, 2, 5–6, 30–32, 60; insured, 3, 49; military, 4, 15, 41, 55–56; noncontributory, 3, 49; pay-as-you-go, 151; policing, 79–80; private, 4, 15, 41, 48–52; qualified, 3, 4; railroaders, 4, 15, 41, 57; and savings, 59–60; state- and local-government, 4, 15, 41, 53–55; trusteed, 3, 49; veterans, 4, 15, 41, 57
Poor, 26, 47; support for, 26
Population. *See* Demography
Population profile, 17–18
Portability of pension credits, 44, 49, 55, 85, 92, 103–104; and individual retirement accounts, 85, 87–88; under private pension plans, 44, 55, 85, 92, 103–104; under social security, 44, 55; under state- and local-government plans, 55
Poverty level. *See* Poor
Private pensions, 4, 15, 41, 48–52, 97–105; adequacy, 51–52, 97–98; compared to social security, 48–50; coverage, 48; dependents benefits, 49; disability benefits, 100; economic importance, 52; funding, 49; integration with social security, 50–51, 102; portability of credits, 49, 103–104; spouse's benefits, 49; termination, 50; variety of, 50
Probate, 65, 72–73, 80; avoiding, 72–73, 80
Productivity, 29–30, 150; decline in, 29; improving, 30; rate of, 29, 41

Qualified plan, 3, 4

Railroaders pensions, 4, 15, 41, 57; and social security, 57
Replacement income, 42, 52, 53, 54, 56; under civil-service pensions, 53; under military pensions, 56; under private pensions, 52; under state- and local-government pensions, 54; under social security, 42–43
Retirement age, 44, 47, 52, 54, 56, 98–99, 131, 135, 152–153; compulsory, 99, 131, 153; early, 44, 98, 128, 135, 153; for federal civil-service pensions, 52; for military pensions, 56; normal, 44, 98, 153; under social security, 44; for state- and local-government pensions, 54

Savings, 29, 30, 42, 59–60; decline in, 29, 30; and pensions, 42, 59–60
Setoff. See Offsets
Social contract, 31
Social security, 1, 4, 15, 41, 42–48; adequacy of benefits, 45–48; dependents benefits, 44–45; disability benefits, 45, 48; fiscal importance, 48; insured under, 44; mother's benefits, 45; nature of, 42–43; portability of credits, 44; quarters of coverage, 44; as replacement income, 42–43, 45–47; retirement age, 44; and self-employed, 43–44; as social insurance, 42–43; spouse's benefits, 44, 45; tax, 16, 44, 48, 151
Spouse, 44, 45, 53, 66, 87; absent, 66; under federal civil-service pensions, 53; divorced, 44; under ERISA, 91–92; IRA for, 87; self-sufficient, 66; under social security, 44, 45; surviving, 45
SSI. See Supplemental security income
State- and local-government pensions, 4, 15, 41, 53–55, 151; adequacy, 54; deficiencies, 55; economic importance, 54–55; general coverage, 54; limited coverage, 54; and social security, 53–54; variety of, 53
Supplemental security income, 15
Support system. See Income maintenance system

Transfer payments. See Income transfers

Unemployed, 25–26; support for, 26
Unemployment compensation, 1, 15, 26
U.S. savings bonds, 73; coowner, 73; pay-on-death, 73

Vesting, 3, 85, 88
Veterans, 24; support for, 24
Veterans pensions, 4, 15, 41, 57, 151; fiscal importance, 57; survivors benefits, 57

Wealth-transmission process, 65, 71–82; bank accounts, 73; charity, 74; common ownership, 74–75; and demography, 77; improving the, 78–81; and income transfers, 76; and inflation, 76; life insurance, 72–73; medical benefits, 73–74; pensions, 73; and taxation, 76
Women, 7, 27–28, 47; self-sufficient, 66; under social security, 47; in work force, 7, 26–28
Workers' compensation, 15
Work force, 1, 26–28; in agriculture, 27; aliens, 28; baby-boom generation, 27; blacks, 26, 28; blue collar, 27; females, 26–28; males, 26–28; in manufacturing, 27; participation rates, 28; in services, 27–28; in trade, 27;

white collar, 26–27; whites, 26, 28

Work place, 135–136, 159; flextime, 136, 159

About the Author

Robert J. Lynn was educated at The Ohio State University and Yale University. He has taught for more than thirty years at Ohio State, where he is presently James W. Shocknessy Professor of Law. Mr. Lynn has been a visiting professor at the University of Illinois, the University of California at Los Angeles (UCLA), and Yale. He is the author of two books, *The Modern Rule Against Perpetuities* (1965), and *An Introduction to Estate Planning* (2d ed. 1978). He has published articles in the Duke, Ohio State, and Yale law journals, and the Arizona, Chicago, Colorado, Georgia, Pennsylvania, Stanford, Texas, Vanderbilt and UCLA law reviews.